A VICTORIAN CHRISTMAS

A VICTORIAN CHRISTMAS

Traditional Recipes and Decorations
for the Festive Season

Evelyn Dix and Jean Smith

Arlington Books
King Street St. James's
London

A VICTORIAN CHRISTMAS: TRADITIONAL
RECIPES AND DECORATIONS FOR THE
FESTIVE SEASON
First Published in England 1987 by
Arlington Books (Publishers) Ltd
15–17 King Street, St James's
London SW1

© *Evelyn Dix & Jean Smith*

Typeset by Inforum, Portsmouth
Printed and Bound by
The Bath Press, Bath

British Library Cataloguing in Publication Data

Dix, Evelyn
A Victorian Christmas:
traditional recipes and decorations for the festive season
1. Christmas cookery
I. Title II. Smith, Jean
641.5'66 TX739

ISBN 0–85140–705–6

CONTENTS

To both our families and close friends

INTRODUCTION

We first became interested in Victorian cooking whilst entertaining visitors from abroad. We wanted to present English dishes which would give a flavour of the unique variety of traditional English fare, determined to dispel any myths that English food is boring and repetitive. Our immediate source was our own substantial family archive of recipes thanks to a Great Grandmother who was a noted cook in her time. Further research revealed a mine of fascinating and varied dishes many of which we felt we could adapt for our own purposes.

What surprised and intrigued us was the range and number of dishes served by the Victorians. Breakfast was, by any standards, a very substantial meal designed to give more than a good start to the day. The limitations of equipment and appliances were, for the more affluent, offset by an abundance of staff. However there were other limitations which are now scarcely apparent: there was still a pronounced seasonal influence on what foodstuffs were available.

The Industrial Revolution which stretched well into the 19th Century had a dramatic effect on the processing and distribution of foodstuffs and paved the way for a much wider choice than ever before. There emerged a society with a greater spread of spending power although it still contained extremes of wealth and poverty. It was a society in which the better off could indulge themselves to the full and for whom mealtimes were events of major importance.

The availability of a wider range of foodstuffs helped to create a market for cookbooks and cooks eagerly began to take advantage of the new opportunities. England began to open its doors to great chefs from the continent. Indeed for many years Queen Victoria and Prince Albert employed a continental chef with a considerable reputation, Charles Elmé Francatelli, who himself wrote *A Cook's Guide*. Other memorable cooks of the period include, of course, Mrs Beeton whose *Book of Household Management* set a precedent in culinary history and Mrs Rundell whose *Domestic Cookery by A Lady* conveys the full flavour of the period.

The highlight of any cook's year is undoubtedly Christmas and for the Victorian cook perhaps even more so. You've only to read Dickens to realise quite how important a part traditional Christmas fare played in the celebration of the season. Even the Cratchitt's sat down to a roast goose and ate 'a pudding, like a speckled cannonball, so hard and firm, blazing in ignited brandy with holly stuck into the top.'

We decided to recreate something of that sumptuousness by celebrating our own Victorian Christmas to include not only the main meals, but also the traditional Victorian drinks, sweetmeats, preserves and cakes that would have been eaten at the time. That was six years ago and the result was such a success that it set a family precedent.

The following year we took it one stage further and provided the atmosphere as well. To add to the sense of the occasion we started to make our own Victorian Christmas decorations for the tree and table and decked the house in true festive style even relegating the television to the broom cupboard. We were encouraged to see if we could pass on the concept to others and out of this grew the idea for our book.

A Victorian Christmas is designed to provide typical meals for you and your guests right through from Christmas Eve to Boxing Day. We have suggested two menus for the main Christmas Day and Boxing Day Dinners, but obviously recipes can be selected from the various sections to create your own. All the traditional Christmas fare is here, all given that additional touch of authenticity by keeping a strict eye on the ingredients that would have been available at the time. All of the dishes included, irrespective of their original source, have been prepared using modern equipment and every attention has been given to ensure that they are easy to follow.

It does involve more time and trouble to prepare a meal of greater range than normal. Readers may like to pick and choose, but there's no doubt that a thoroughly Victorian Christmas is well worth the effort and will prove a memorable occasion for both you and your guests.

Evelyn Dix & Jean Smith

NOTES

All the recipes are adapted from traditional sources. They have been tried and tested by the authors in order to achieve the best results.

CANDIES

For the toffee and sweet recipes it is advisable to use a candy thermometer which can hang in the pan whilst boiling.

CAKES

Cakes freeze well at certain stages of preparation, that is before the finishing touches have been added such as frosting or dusting with icing sugar.

FROZEN CREAM ROSETTES

These are handy for last minute decoration of cakes or desserts.

Have ready a plate or baking tray lined with cooking foil, non-stick pure baking parchment paper or waxed paper.

Place whipped double cream which has had a little sugar added to it in a piping bag fitted with a star nozzle and, with a little space between them, press out rosettes onto the base lining. Open freeze. When frozen remove the rosettes from the base lining (a spatula is a good tool to use for this purpose as it is important not to touch them with your hands) and place in a rigid container between layers of waxed paper then store for up to three months. When required for use remove as before with a spatula.

HERBS

We have given quantities mainly for dried herbs in the recipes because of the time of year. If fresh herbs are available use double the quantity of fresh herbs to dry.

ORANGE AND ROSEWATER

Where we specify orange or rose water it must be triple strength.

OVENS

As these vary we have used the term approximately for cooking times.

PASTRY

Pastry does require a cold surface and is best rolled out on a marble pastry slab using a marble rolling pin.

SPOON MEASUREMENTS

All spoon measurements are level.

WEIGHTS AND MEASURES

Imperial and metric. Use just one of the sets of weights and measures for any given recipe, do not combine the two.

YEAST

We have given quantities for fresh yeast in our recipes. If using dried yeast halve the quantity as dried yeast is more concentrated.

CHRISTMAS EVE

*To greet guests arriving late on Christmas Eve
we recommend serving hot Mince Pies and Great Grandmother's
Christmas Plum Cake together with one of the Christmas drinks
on our list. If they are still in need!
Follow up with the Francatelli 'Night Cap'
which is with the Mince Pies recipe.*

GREAT GRANDMOTHER'S CHRISTMAS MINCE PIES
WITH ORANGE PASTRY

Hot mince pies are indispensable at Christmas.

On Christmas Eve it is an old English tradition to hand them round to calling carol singers. After returning from the midnight service they are served with perhaps, a hot punch or maybe Francatelli's Nightcap: Half a pint of strong ale, a wineglass of brandy, a few drops of essence of cloves, 4 lumps of sugar, make hot, drink slowly—and make haste into bed.

We are using an old family recipe for these mince pies. Replace orange water with water if a more conventional pastry is required.

FAIRLY HOT OVEN
Gas Mark 6   400°F 200°C

Approximately 15 minutes

Patty pans
Makes about 18

INGREDIENTS

for Rich Short Crust Pastry:

8 oz (225g) plain flour
pinch salt
6 oz (170g) butter-cut into small pieces
1 tablespoon caster sugar
1 large egg yolk
2–3 tablespoons orange water

1 lb (450g) mincemeat
1 small egg–beaten
milk

METHOD

Blend egg yolk and orange water. Sift the flour with the salt in a large bowl. Add the butter and rub in with the fingertips until the mixture resembles fine breadcrumbs. Mix in the sugar then using a round-bladed knife quickly mix in sufficient egg yolk and orange water to form a firm dough. Turn out onto a

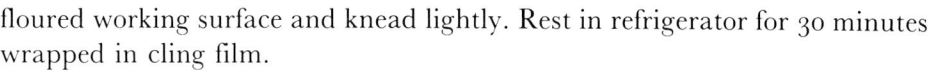

floured working surface and knead lightly. Rest in refrigerator for 30 minutes wrapped in cling film.

PRE-HEAT OVEN

Roll half of the dough our fairly thinly on a floured working surface, then cut out 18 × 2½″ (6 cm) diameter circles with a pastry cutter. Gather up the trimmings and add them to the second half of the dough. Roll this half of the dough out a little thinner than the first half and cut out 18 × 3″ (7.6 cm) diameter circles. Line patty pans with the larger dough circles and spoon a portion of mincemeat into the base of each; brush the edges of the smaller dough circles with beaten egg and place on top to form lids, lightly pressing edges together to seal. Make a small hole in each lid and then brush with a little milk. Place in the oven and bake until golden. Cool slightly in the tins before carefully transferring to wire racks to cool.

Store in an airtight container.

Serve hot or cold sprinkled with caster sugar or sifted icing sugar.

Note: We make a small foil funnel and just before serving insert the funnel into the hole on the top of each mince pie; we then add a drop of brandy via the funnel.

MINCEMEAT

Yield about 8 lb

INGREDIENTS

1 lb (450g) muscatel raisins—stoned and halved
2 lb (900g) currants
8 oz (225g) sultanas
1¼ lb (570g) cooking apples
1¼ lb (570g) moist brown sugar
12 oz (340g) suet—finely grated
4 oz (100g) mixed candied peel-finely sliced
2 lemons—juice and grated rind
2 oranges—juice and grated rind
3 oz (85g) almonds-cut into slivers
2 tablespoons mixed spice
½ grated nutmeg
½ pint (275ml) brandy
2 tablespoons port

METHOD

Core, peel and grate the apples. Mix all ingredients well together then pack into sterilized jars; cover with wax discs then place on lids. Store in a cool dark place.

Note: Prepare this at least one month before required to allow mincemeat to mature.

GREAT GRANDMOTHER'S
CHRISTMAS PLUM CAKE

MODERATE OVEN
Gas Mark 3   325°F 160°C
After 2 hours reduce to:
Gas Mark 2   300°F 150°C

Approximately 6 hours

Butter a round cake tin 12" (30 cm) and line with 5 sheets of greaseproof paper. Tie 2 sheets of brown paper around the cake tin to stand well above the rim. Place 2 sheets of brown paper on the oven shelf for the cake to stand on. After 2 hours reduce the heat and very quickly place a sheet of greaseproof paper over the top of the cake.

INGREDIENTS

1½ lb (700g) plain flour
1 teaspoon salt
½ oz (10g) each ground cinnamon, cloves and nutmeg
1½ lb (700g) currants
1 lb (450g) dried candied cherries—quartered
8 oz (225g) candied citron peel
8 oz (225g) candied lemon peel
8 oz (225g) candied orange peel
1 lemon—grated rind
2 oranges—grated rind
1½ lb (700g) soft butter
1 lb (450g) soft brown sugar
8 large eggs
8 oz (225g) ground almonds
½ pint (275ml) brandy
extra brandy—to pour over finished cake

Note: Dried Candied Cherries are normally used in this recipe (see Candied, Crystallized and Glacé Fruits recipe page 156). If fresh cherries are not available to candy purchased glacé cherries can be used in the following manner. Place a wire rack over a baking tray to catch the drips then lay the glacé cherries on the rack; place in the oven on the lowest possible heat and leave for about 4 hours or until the cherries are no longer sticky. The cherries are now ready to be quartered and used in the Christmas Plum Cake recipe.

METHOD

PRE-HEAT OVEN

Sift together the flour, salt and cinnamon. Shred the peel finely.

Place the flour mixture in a bowl and stir in one third of the dried fruit and the grated lemon and orange rinds.

Cream the butter in a very large bowl then add the sugar and beat thoroughly until light and fluffy. Beat in the eggs one at a time. Fold in the ground almonds and half of the flour mixture. Add the brandy and then the remaining flour mixture. Stir in the remaining fruit. Turn mixture into the prepared cake tin and smooth over the top of the mixture making a slight hollow in the centre (this helps to give a flat surface to the finished cake). Sprinkle surface of cake mixture with a little water to keep the top of the cake soft.

Place in the oven and cook for 2 hours; reduce heat then open the oven door and quickly cover cake with a sheet of greaseproof paper (resting the paper on the raised rim of the paper tied around the outside of the tin). Close the oven door carefully.

Test to see if the cake is cooked by inserting a skewer into the centre, if it comes out clean the cake is finished. Another test is to listen to the cake. If it is silent it is finished.

Remove cake from the oven and leave to cool in the tin. Turn cake out onto a wire rack and remove greaseproof paper. Prick the top of the cake with a skewer and sprinkle over three tablespoons of brandy. Wrap the cake in two sheets of greaseproof paper then cover and seal with foil. Store in an airtight container.

Note: Make this cake at least 3 months in advance as all rich fruit cakes improve with keeping. This gives the cake time to mature. About every 3 weeks unwrap the cake and sprinkle 3 tablespoons of brandy over the top; rewrap and place back in an airtight container.

ALMOND PASTE FOR PLUM CAKE

INGREDIENTS

3 lb (1.35 kg) icing sugar—sifted
2 lb (900 g) ground almonds
3 large eggs
1 large egg yolk
1 teaspoon lemon juice
1 teaspoon almond essence
1 tablespoon orange water
cornflour
warm apricot jam—sieved

METHOD

Mix together the icing sugar and ground almonds in a large bowl. Beat together the eggs with the extra egg yolk and add to the icing sugar mixture with the lemon juice, almond essence and orange water. There should be enough liquid to form a stiff paste. Knead with the hands until smooth.

Use masking tape to attach the baking parchment firmly onto the working surface. This stops it slipping about whilst you are rolling the almond paste out. Dust the parchment with cornflour. Divide the almond paste in half, form a ball with one half then divide the remaining almond paste in half and form two sausage shapes. Place the ball of almond paste on the prepared baking parchment and flatten it out with your hands then dust it lightly with cornflour; dust a rolling pin with cornflour and roll out the almond paste to fit the top of the cake. Coat the almond paste with a thin layer of warm apricot jam. Turn the cake upside down onto the paste and press to flatten the top, carefully turn the cake over and place to one side. Clear away any cake crumbs from the baking parchment and dust again with cornflour. Measure around the cake then place the two sausage shapes of almond paste on the baking parchment, dust the rolling pin with cornflour and roll out each piece of almond paste to the depth of the cake and a sufficient length to go half way round. Coat the strips of almond paste with warm apricot jam then pick up the cake and place on the almond strips rolling it round to attach the almond paste. Place the cake right side up and lightly roll the top once more. Run a straight-sided jar around the side to give a flat finish. Place the cake on a silver board, then cover with greaseproof paper and allow the paste to dry out for about 6 days before icing.

ROYAL ICING FOR PLUM CAKE

INGREDIENTS

4 lb (1.8 kg) icing sugar—sifted
8 large egg whites
1 tablespoon lemon juice
1 tablespoon glycerine

METHOD

Whisk the egg whites until frothy in a large bowl then gradually whisk in the icing sugar until the mixture is stiff enough to stand up in peaks. Whisk in the lemon juice and then the glycerine.

Cover the cake with the icing then using the tip of a knife quickly pull the icing up into little peaks to create a snow effect. Decorate with chosen ornaments.

CHRISTMAS
BREAKFAST

*The Victorians expected a substantial meal to start the day
so we have included a selection of recipes from which
a choice of perhaps four dishes can be made.*

CROQUETTES OF TURKEY
Adapted from Mrs Beeton's *Book of Household Management* (1861)

INGREDIENTS

to every:
8 oz (225 g) cold turkey meat—finely minced
allow:
2 oz (50 g) lean ham or bacon—finely minced
½ pint (280 ml) gravy—made from the bones and trimmings
2 oz (50 g) butter
2 shallots—minced
1 tablespoon flour
2 large egg yolks—beaten
1 large egg—beaten
breadcrumbs
oil for frying

METHOD

Mince the meat finely with the ham or bacon. Make a gravy with the bones and trimmings; season. Melt the butter in a saucepan, stir in the shallots and the flour. Add the minced meat mixture and half a pint of gravy. Bring to the boil and when just boiled, remove from the heat and stir in two egg yolks. Leave the mixture to cool. Shape mixture, using clean floured hands, into sausage shapes. Coat the croquettes with beaten egg before rolling in the breadcrumbs. Fry until golden brown. Drain on kitchen paper towels.

Serve with grilled bacon rolls. See page 93.

GREAT GRANDMOTHER'S
CARAWAY SEED SCONES

HOT OVEN
Gas Mark 7   450°F 230°C

Approximately 10 minutes

A non-stick baking tray
Makes 12 small scones

INGREDIENTS

8 oz (225 g) plain flour
½ teaspoon bicarbonate of soda
1 teaspoon cream of tartar—½ teaspoon if sour milk is used
¼ teaspoon salt
1½ oz (35g) butter—firm cut into small pieces
1 tablespoon caster sugar
1 tablespoon caraway seeds
scant ¼ pint (150 ml) milk
extra milk—for brushing scones

METHOD

PRE-HEAT OVEN

Sift flour, bicarbonate of soda, cream of tartar and salt in a large bowl. Rub in the butter until the mixture resembles breadcrumbs. Mix in the caster sugar and caraway seeds then gradually add the milk and mix to a soft, but not wet, dough using a round-bladed knife. Knead lightly on a floured working surface and roll out to a ½" (1.3 cm) thickness. Cut-out rounds with a 2" (5 cm) pastry cutter and place rounds on a non-stick baking tray; brush with milk and place in the preheated oven; bake until well risen and golden. Cool on a wire rack.

Serve scones with butter.

Note: These are best eaten on the day they are baked. If sour milk is used a better result is achieved.

BEEF, MINCED, WITH POACHED EGGS

Adapted from Mrs Beeton's *Book of Household Management* (1911)

Serves 4

INGREDIENTS

1 oz (25 g) butter
1 large onion—finely chopped
1 oz (25 g) flour
½ pint (275 ml) stock
1 lb (450 g) underdone roast beef—diced
1 tablespoon mushroom ketchup
1 tablespoon Worcestershire sauce
seasoning
4 large eggs
8 slices toast-cut into small triangular shapes

METHOD

Melt the butter in a saucepan and fry the onion until lightly browned, sprinkle in the flour and brown slightly, then add the stock and boil for 3 minutes. Add the meat, ketchup, Worcestershire sauce and seasoning. Keep hot.

Meanwhile, poach the eggs and prepare the toast. When ready to serve, turn the mince out onto a hot dish, place the eggs on top and surround the base with the pieces of toast.

BACON AND MACARONI
Adapted from Mrs Beeton's *Book of Household Management* (1911)

Serves 4–6

INGREDIENTS

8 oz (225 g) macaroni
8 oz (225 g) streaky bacon—diced finely
1 pint (570 ml) white stock
2 oz (50 g) butter
large pinch grated nutmeg
seasoning

METHOD

Put the macaroni into a saucepan of lightly-salted, boiling water. Boil rapidly for 5 minutes, then drain well. Pour the stock into a saucepan and bring to the boil; put in the drained macaroni and cook until just tender. Lightly fry the bacon. Drain the macaroni once more then add it to the bacon with the butter, grated nutmeg and seasoning. Stir gently over a medium heat until the macaroni acquires a nice brown colour. Turn out onto a hot dish and serve.

FRIED PARSLEY

INGREDIENTS

fresh parsley—washed and thoroughly dried, stalks removed
oil

METHOD

Heat the oil in a chip pan to 375°F 190°C. Put the prepared parsley in the frying basket and immerse in the hot fat. Remove when the hissing stops; it should be green and crisp. Drain on white kitchen paper towels and serve at once.

DEVILLED BONES

For left-over roast meats, poultry and game

INGREDIENTS

2 oz (50 g) butter—softened
1 oz (25 g) flour
1 teaspoon English mustard powder
1 teaspoon French mustard
1 tablespoon chutney
1 tablespoon Worcestershire Sauce
12 oz (350 g) left over cold meat, poultry or game—cut into fingers

METHOD

Cream the butter and flour to a smooth paste. Then mix the paste and remaining ingredients together thoroughly. Spread thickly over fingers of cooked meats, poultry or game and grill until crisp and golden brown.

Note: The authors wish to express their thanks to the manufacturers of LEA & PERRINS Worcestershire Sauce for supplying this recipe.

HAM OMELETTE

Adapted from Mrs Beeton's *Book of Household Management* (1861)

Serves 4

INGREDIENTS

2 tablespoons lean minced ham
6 large eggs—separated
ground black pepper
5 oz (125 g) butter

METHOD

Fry the ham for 2 minutes in 1 oz (25g) of butter. Put 6 egg yolks and 3 whites in a large bowl and beat well seasoning with pepper, then stir in 2 oz (50g) of the butter (broken into small pieces) and the ham.

PRE-HEAT GRILL

Put the remaining butter into an omelette pan and when it bubbles, pour in the egg mixture and fry over a gentle heat for 4–6 minutes. When the eggs are set, place the omelette under a hot grill until lightly coloured. Slip omelette onto a hot plate and serve.

KIDNEYS GRILLED

Adapted from Mrs Beeton's *Book of Household Management* (1861)

INGREDIENTS

lambs kidneys
melted butter
seasoning

METHOD

PRE-HEAT GRILL

Remove any hard fat and the transparent skin, slice the kidneys lengthways and cut out the central core; brush each portion of kidney with melted butter and season. Grill for about 3 minutes on each side and serve hot.

GAME DEVILLED

Adapted from Mrs Beeton's *Book of Household Management* (1911)

INGREDIENTS

for Devilled Butter:

1½ oz (35 g) butter
1 teaspoon chutney
½ teaspoon anchovy essence
½ teaspoon lemon juice
large pinch cayenne pepper

remains of cold game—skinned, boned and cut into neat pieces
clarified butter for frying
salt

METHOD

Knead the ingredients for Devilled Butter together then rub them through a fine sieve. Fry the prepared game in hot butter until well browned, then sprinkle with salt. Spread each piece of fried and salted game with the prepared devilled butter. Place on a hot serving dish.

Garnish with fried parsley.

BAKED WHITE HERRINGS

Adapted from Mrs Beeton's *Book of Household Management* (1861)

COOL OVEN
Gas Mark 1   275°F 140°C

Approximately 2 hours

1 piedish

INGREDIENTS

12 fresh herrings
4 bayleaves
10 cloves
10 allspice
a small blade of mace
cayenne pepper
salt
vinegar

METHOD

PRE-HEAT OVEN

Wash the herrings. Cut off the heads and split them open to remove the gut and backbone. Roll them up beginning with the neck of the fish and sprinkle over the other ingredients. Cover the fish with sufficient vinegar to fill up the dish and bake in a very slow oven for 2 hours. When done let the fish remain in the dish in which they were cooked until ready to serve.

SARDINE TOAST

Adapted from Mrs Beeton's *Book of Household Management* (1911)

Serves 12

INGREDIENTS

1½ oz (35 g) butter
6 tablespoons milk
12 sardines
3 teaspoons anchovy essence
large pinch cayenne pepper
6 egg yolks
12 squares toast

METHOD

Skin, bone and chop the sardines coarsely. Put the butter and milk into a saucepan; when hot add the prepared sardines, anchovy essence, cayenne pepper and then add the egg yolks. Stir over a gentle heat until the mixture thickens. Do not boil or it will curdle. Serve hot on well-buttered toast.

POACHED EGGS WITH CREAM

Adapted from Mrs Beeton's *Book of Household Management* (1861)

Serves 4

INGREDIENTS

1 pint (570 ml) water
2 tablespoons vinegar
1 teaspoon salt
4 large eggs
2 fl oz (50 ml) single cream
seasoning
1 oz (25 g) butter—broken into small pieces

METHOD

Put the water, vinegar and salt into a frying pan and bring to the boil. Break the eggs into a cup and slide them gently into the frying pan without breaking the yolks. Simmer them for no longer than 4 minutes and then lift them out with a slice and place them on a hot dish. Empty the frying pan and put in the cream and seasoning to taste; bring to boiling point; then add the butter, broken into small pieces; stir until butter melts then pour the cream mixture over the eggs. Serve them immediately.

POTTED BLOATERS

Adapted from the *Cook's Guide* by Charles Elmé Francatelli (1888)

Serves 12

INGREDIENTS

3½ lb (1.6 kg) fresh cured Yarmouth bloaters
6 oz (175 g) clarified butter
1 blade of mace
1 teaspoon anchovy essence
pinch cayenne pepper
additional clarified butter—for sealing potted bloaters

METHOD

Remove heads, tails and backbones from bloaters and immerse in scalding water to remove the skins. Place in a saucepan with the clarified butter, mace, anchovy and cayenne pepper. Simmer for 10 minutes. Remove and pound in a morter, then rub through a course sieve. Use this preparation to fill small ramekin dishes which must be covered over with clarified butter to seal contents. Keep in a cool place.

Note: Smoked salmon or dried haddock treated in the same manner as bloaters will furnish other delicate relishes for the breakfast or the tea table.

POTTED PHEASANT

Adapted from the *Cook's Guide* by Charles Elmé Francatelli (1888)

Serves 12

INGREDIENTS

1 roasted pheasant—meat removed from the bone
5 tablespoons sherry
5 tablespoons mushroom ketchup
4 shallots
1 bay leaf
¼ teaspoon dried thyme
2 oz (50 g) cooked ham
1½ pints (850 ml) good gravy
6 oz (175 g) clarified butter
salt and cayenne pepper to taste
additional clarified butter for sealing potted pheasant

METHOD

Place pheasant meat, sherry, mushroom ketchup, shallots, bay leaf, thyme, ham and the gravy in a saucepan. Boil until the gravy is a glaze then strain off into a basin. Remove bay leaf, chop and then pound the meat mixture in a mortar into a smooth pulp; add the glaze and the clarified butter, salt and cayenne pepper; pound all together then fill small pots (or jars) with the pheasant mixture and pour the extra clarified butter over the surface to seal the contents. Keep in a cool place.

POTTED CHICKEN

FAIRLY HOT OVEN
Gas Mark 6   400°F 200°C

Approximately 1¼–1½ hours

1 pint dish (570 ml)
Serves 4–6

INGREDIENTS

2½ lb (1 kg) roasting chicken
4 oz (100 g) streaky bacon—rind removed
¼ pint (150 ml) chicken stock
2 tablespoons Worcestershire Sauce
2 oz (50 g) butter—melted
2 tablespoons fresh parsley—chopped
seasoning
hot buttered toast

METHOD

Place chicken and bacon in a roasting pan, pour over stock and cook for 1¼–1½ hours. Remove chicken and bacon and reserve stock.

Strip meat from chicken and mince chicken and bacon. Mix together with Worcestershire Sauce, butter and 4 tablespoons reserved chicken stock. Add parsley and seasoning. Press mixture into dish and chill. When set, serve with hot buttered toast.

Note: The authors wish to express their thanks to the manufacturers of LEA & PERRINS Worcestershire Sauce for this recipe.

POTTED LOBSTER

Adapted from the *Cook's Guide* by Charles Elmé Francatelli (1888)

Serves 4

INGREDIENTS

1 lb (450 g) fresh boiled lobster
1 teaspoon anchovy essence
pinch cayenne pepper
powdered mace
4 oz (100 g) clarified butter
additional clarified butter to seal

METHOD

Pound the lobster meat, pith and coral to a smooth pulp then add the anchovy essence, cayenne pepper, mace and the clarified butter; pound all together thoroughly and put it into pots or jars. Smooth over the surface and cover with extra clarified butter to seal the contents.

Keep in a cool place.

Note: Another method is to pound only one half of the lobster meat. Cut the remainder into small squares and mix in with the preparation.

WOODCOCK ROASTED

These birds are dressed without being drawn. Woodcock is hung until the feathers pull out easily above the tail

FAIRLY HOT OVEN
Gas Mark 7   425°F 220°C

Approximately 15–20 minutes

INGREDIENTS

12 woodcock
12 strips of fatty bacon
butter—melted
12 slices toast

flour for browning

METHOD

PRE-HEAT OVEN

Wipe the birds well outside; truss with the legs close to the body and the feet pressing upon the thighs. Skin the neck and the head then bring the beak round under the wing. Put the toast in a roasting tin; place a wire rack over the toast then place the birds on the rack. Brush the birds with melted butter and tie a strip of bacon over the breast of each bird.

Baste frequently. Take the birds out of the oven 5 minutes before the end of the roasting period and remove the trussing; take off the strips of bacon fat. Dust the birds with flour and return to the oven to finish roasting. Serve each bird on a slice of the toast. Keep warm until required.

Note: To spit roast hang the birds on the spit feet downwards, placing the toast in the dripping pan to catch the tails. Baste frequently. Remove from spit after approximately 15 minutes, discard the trussing and bacon fat.

EXTRACT OF GAME FOR GRAVY

INGREDIENTS

remains of game
1 oz (25 g) butter
4 shallots—chopped
1 bay leaf
½ teaspoon dried thyme
4 cloves
5 peppercorns
1¾ pints (1 litre) stock or water

METHOD

Put bones and any remains of game in a saucepan with the butter, shallots, bay leaf, dried thyme, cloves and peppercorns; fry until they become brown; add the stock or water; boil for 15 minutes then strain through a sieve.

SALMON KEDGEREE

Serves 6–8

INGREDIENTS

3 oz (75 g) butter
12 oz (350 g) rice—well boiled and drained
grated nutmeg
seasoning
1 lb (450 g) tin salmon—drained, boned and divided into large flakes
2 large eggs—hard boiled and roughly chopped
fresh parsley—finely chopped

METHOD

Melt the butter in a large saucepan and add the cooked rice; heat through. Stir in the nutmeg with seasoning to taste then very gently stir in the flaked salmon and heat through until hot.

Turn out onto a large, hot, serving dish and pile high. Garnish with chopped eggs and parsley.

SPICY BEEF CECILS

Cecils are the early 19th Century name for rounds of minced beef flavoured with anchovies and lemon. Originally Cecils were egg-and-breadcrumbed and deep fried.

Serves 4

INGREDIENTS

1 lb (450 g) minced beef
1 medium onion—finely chopped
2 oz (50 g) fresh white breadcrumbs
½ lemon—grated rind
4 anchovy fillets—chopped
1 tablespoon fresh parsley—chopped
seasoning
1 tablespoon Worcestershire Sauce
1 large egg—beaten
1 oz (25 g) butter—for frying

METHOD

Combine all ingredients, except butter, in a bowl and mix well. Divide mixture into 12 pieces and shape into flat round cakes. Heat butter in a pan and fry Cecils for 7–10 minutes, turning once, until golden brown. Drain well on white kitchen paper towels. Serve with brown gravy or tomato sauce.

Note: The authors wish to express their thanks to the manufacturers of LEA & PERRINS Worcestershire Sauce for supplying this recipe.

SAVOURY DUCKS

Savoury Ducks, also called Faggots, originally were served with fried eggs for breakfast

MODERATE OVEN
Gas Mark 4   350°F   180°C

Approximately 30 minutes
Serves 4

INGREDIENTS

1 lb (450 g) pigs liver
2 large onions
6 oz (175 g) fresh white breadcrumbs
2 oz (50 g) shredded suet
1 tablespoon Worcestershire Sauce
½ teaspoon dried sage
seasoning

for the Gravy:

1 oz (25 g) lard
1 onion—sliced
2 carrots—grated
1 oz (25 g) flour
¾ pint (425 ml) beef stock
2 teaspoons Worcestershire Sauce
seasoning

METHOD

Mince the pig's liver and onions and mix together with the breadcrumbs, suet, Worcestershire Sauce, sage and seasoning. Divide mixture into 8 and shape roughly into balls. Place in a prepared ovenproof dish and bake, uncovered, for approximately 30 minutes. Remove from oven and turn each Savoury Duck over. Meanwhile, for the gravy, heat lard in a pan and add onion and carrot. Fry gently for 5 minutes. Stir in flour and cook for 1 minute. Remove from heat and blend in stock and Worcestershire Sauce. Return to heat and bring to the boil, stirring. Simmer for 10 minutes and strain. Season. Pour over Savoury Ducks and return dish to oven. Cook for approximately 20 minutes.

Note: The authors wish to express their thanks to the manufacturers of LEA & PERRINS Worcestershire Sauce for supplying this recipe.

SCRAMBLED EGGS WITH KIPPERS

Serves 4

INGREDIENTS

2 oz (50 g) butter
4 large eggs
2 tablespoons single cream
seasoning
1 teaspoon fresh parsley—finely chopped

4 kippers
1 oz (25 g) butter—cut into four portions
ground black pepper

METHOD

PRE-HEAT GRILL

Lightly beat the single cream and eggs together. Melt the butter in a saucepan then add the egg mixture and stir over a low heat until the eggs begin to set. Turn out onto a hot serving dish and sprinkle with the parsley.

Lightly butter a length of cooking foil and place foil in the grill pan. Trim the kippers and lay them on the buttered foil with the skin side of the kippers on the top; dot with pieces of butter and grill for about 1 minute. Turn kippers over, dot with remaining butter and grill for about 4 minutes. Remove from the grill pan and arrange on a hot serving plate; place a portion of butter on each kipper and season with ground black pepper.

GREAT GRANDMOTHER'S QUICK BREAKFAST BUNS

HOT OVEN
Gas Mark 8   450°F 230°C

Approximately 15 minutes

1 large baking tray—lightly buttered
Makes 12

INGREDIENTS

1 lb (450 g) plain flour
1 tablespoon baking powder
1 teaspoon salt
1 teaspoon granulated sugar
1 oz (25 g) butter
1 oz (25 g) fresh yeast
½ pint (275 ml) lukewarm milk
1 large egg

METHOD

Sift together the flour, baking powder and salt in a large bowl. Add the granulated sugar and rub in the butter. Whisk together the fresh yeast with half of the milk. Blend the remaining milk with beaten egg. Combine the milk mixtures and add to the large bowl to form a soft dough. Turn dough out onto a floured working surface and knead until smooth and elastic. Divide dough into 12 portions, roll into balls and place on a baking tray. Cover with greased cling film and leave in a warm place until they double in size.

PRE-HEAT OVEN

Dust buns with a little flour and place in the oven. Bake until golden brown. Cool on wire racks.

SODA BREAD

FAIRLY HOT OVEN
Gas Mark 6   400°F 200°C

Approximately 30 minutes

1 baking tray—lightly dusted with flour

INGREDIENTS

1 lb (450 g) plain white flour
1 teaspoon salt
2 teaspoons bicarbonate of soda
1 teaspoon sugar
2 oz (50 g) butter
½ pint (275 ml) buttermilk

METHOD

PRE-HEAT OVEN

Sift together the flour, salt and bicarbonate of soda. Place the mixture in a large bowl with the sugar then add the butter and rub in until the mixture resembles fine breadcrumbs. Add the milk and mix to a soft dough; turn dough out onto a floured surface and knead lightly until smooth. Shape into a 7″ (18 cm) round. Place on prepared tray and mark into 4 wedges with a sharp knife. Bake until the base sounds hollow when tapped.

Wrap the bread in a clean dry tea towel as soon as it is taken from the oven and leave in the tea towel until required.

Note: This bread is best eaten while it is still warm.

WORCESTERSHIRE TOASTS

Serves 4

INGREDIENTS
1 dessert apple
4 oz (100 g) mature cheddar cheese, grated
1 tablespoon Worcestershire Sauce
seasoning
4 large thick slices white buttered toast
4 rashers streaky bacon, chopped and rind removed

METHOD
PRE-HEAT GRILL TO MODERATELY HOT

Core, peel and finely chop the apple. Mix together with the cheese, Worcestershire sauce and seasoning. Spread the apple mixture onto the buttered toast and top with chopped bacon. Grill for about 4 to 5 minutes until bacon is crispy and cheese is golden brown.

Note: The authors wish to express their thanks to the manufacturers of LEA & PERRINS Worcestershire Sauce for supplying the above recipe.

ROAST PHEASANT

Choose young birds with pliable feet and a supple breastbone for roasting. The pheasant should be hung until the feathers pull out easily above the tail. If a ready-prepared frozen bird is being used please read instructions on the wrapper very carefully before defrosting.

HOT OVEN
Gas Mark 7   425°F 220°C

Approximately 20 minutes per pound (450 g)

INGREDIENTS

1 pheasant
2 rashers streaky bacon
3 oz (75 g) butter
seasoning
flour for browning

METHOD

Wipe bird inside and out with a clean damp cloth. Season and place 1 oz (25g) of butter in the cavity; this helps to keep the bird moist. Truss the bird and cover the breast with the bacon rashers. Heat the remaining butter in a roasting tin. Put in the bird and baste well. Baste frequently during roasting. Remove bacon rashers and trussing for the last 5 minutes of the roasting period; dust breast with flour and baste again before placing back in the oven.

CHRISTMAS LUNCH

*In anticipation of the 'feast' to be served
in the evening we have provided a choice of recipes
to be served cold—a meal at which the guests
can use their own discretion.*

COLD ROAST BEEF

Sirloin on the bone with the undercut or fillet is excellent for roasting, so too is Rib roast. They can be boned and rolled but the meat is juicier and has more flavour on the bone. The joint should not weigh less than 4 lb on the bone as small joints tend to dry up. The beef should be well hung with creamy fat and purplish red flesh.

FAIRLY HOT OVEN
Gas Mark 5   375°F 190°C

Rare: Approximately 15 minutes to the pound (450 g) and 15 minutes over
Well done: Approximately 20 minutes to the pound (450 g) and 30 minutes over

Joint on the bone: Allow 8–12 oz (225–340 g) per person
Boned and rolled joints: Allow 6–8 oz (170–225 g) per person

INGREDIENTS
joint of beef on the bone or boned and rolled
3 tablespoons beef dripping
2 oz (50 g) flour
1 teaspoon mustard powder
1 teaspoon salt
½ teaspoon ground black pepper
2 oz (50 g) soft butter

METHOD
PRE-HEAT OVEN

Place the roasting tin in the pre-heated oven with the dripping. Coat the joint with the flour mixed with mustard powder, salt & pepper. When the dripping is smoking remove the roasting tin from the oven and place a grid on the base of the tin. Stand the joint on its edge upon the grid. Baste it well, this will seal in the juices. Dab small knobs of butter on the top of the joint; place in the oven and baste from time to time.

When the joint is cooked remove it from the oven. Take the joint out of the roasting tin and place it on a plate. Leave until cold.

To serve carve a few slices off the joint and arrange them around the remainder of the joint on a large platter. Serve with horseradish sauce, English mustard and various pickles.

COLD BOILED HAM

Allow 20 minutes per pound (450 g)

Serves 12

INGREDIENTS
6–7 lb (3 kg) ham—on the bone
2 tablespoons vinegar
½ head celery—chopped
1 small carrot—sliced
1 small onion—sliced
1 tablespoon light brown sugar
1 tablespoon vinegar
6 black peppercorns
1 bay leaf
½ pint (275 ml) browned breadcrumbs
paper ruffle

METHOD

Soak ham overnight in the vinegar and enough cold water to cover it. Wash ham thoroughly and if necessary lightly scrape the surface. Place the ham in a large saucepan with the prepared vegetables, sugar, peppercorns and bay leaf, then cover with cold water. Cover with a lid and bring to the boil and then remove any scum. The water should be allowed to simmer until the ham is tender. Whilst simmering remove any further scum which may appear.

Leave the cooked ham in the water until nearly cold. Then remove and strip off the skin and cover with breadcrumbs. Place a paper ruffle round the knuckle.

To serve place ham on a ham stand if possible. Using a very thin, sharp knife commence carving at the knuckle end cutting thin slices at a shallow angle away from the thick part of the ham. Take the knife right down to the bone.

PARTRIDGES IN ASPIC JELLY

Young partridges with yellowish legs and pliable feet should be chosen for roasting. The partridge should be hung until the feathers pull out easily above the tail. The French red-legged partridge is a drier bird and is considered to have less flavour than the English. It is sometimes possible to buy an oven ready frozen partridge. Please read instructions on the wrapper very carefully before defrosting.

FAIRLY HOT OVEN
Gas Mark 7   425°F   220°C

Approximately 30–40 minutes

Serves 8

INGREDIENTS

4 partridges
6 oz (150 g) soft butter
1 tablespoon lemon juice
ground black pepper
2½ fl oz (60 ml) dry white wine
4 strips pork fat
1¾ pints (1 litre) aspic jelly—see recipe pp. 113
celery leaves

METHOD
PRE-HEAT OVEN

Wipe each bird inside and out with a clean damp cloth. Blend together the butter, lemon juice and pepper. Place a little of the butter mixture into the cavity of each bird. Truss the birds; put them in a roasting tin (do not let the birds touch one another) and then pour in the wine. Spread the remaining butter mixture over the tops of the birds; cover the breasts with the strips of pork fat. Baste frequently. Remove the strips of pork fat and trussing for the last 10 minutes of roasting time and dust the birds lightly with flour; roast until juices run clear when thighs are pierced with a skewer. Leave birds until they are cold.

Stand wire racks on a baking sheet and place partridges on them. Coat the birds with a layer of aspic jelly. When this layer has set decorate the partridges with blanched celery leaves then coat with a second layer of aspic jelly.

To serve place partridges on a serving platter and decorate with chopped aspic jelly.

Note: Aspic jelly can also be bought in powdered form.

SCOTCH EGGS

INGREDIENTS
6 large hard boiled eggs
flour
12 oz (350 g) sausage meat
1 large egg—beaten
6 oz (175 g) dried breadcrumbs

METHOD
Shell each hard boiled egg and roll in flour then cover with sausage meat pressing firmly to give a smooth finish. Coat with beaten egg then roll in dried breadcrumbs. Fry in smoking hot oil until golden brown; drain on white kitchen paper towels then leave to cool on a wire rack.

Serve cold. Cut each egg in half lengthways and arrange cut side uppermost on a serving plate.

OLD ENGLISH PORK AND RAISIN PIE

Adapted from Cassell's *New Universal Cookery Book* by Lizzie Heritage (1896)

MODERATE OVEN
Gas Mark 4   350°F   180°C

Approximately 2¼–2½ hours

A large loaf tin
Serves 6–8

INGREDIENTS

for the pastry:

1½ lb (700 g) plain flour
¼ teaspoon salt
6 oz (150 g) lard
½ pint (275 ml) boiling water

for the filling:

2½ lb (1 kg) pork loin, neck or foreloin cut into small cubes
1½ teaspoons dried marjoram
1½ teaspoons dried sage
½ teaspoon dried thyme
1 tablespoon lemon juice
1 tablespoon water
seasoning
4 oz (100 g) stoned raisins
1 large egg—beaten
½ pint (275 ml) aspic jelly—see recipe page 113

METHOD

PRE-HEAT OVEN

Sift together the flour and salt in a large bowl. Melt lard in half a pint of boiling water then gradually beat into the flour mixture; knead into a compact dough. Roll out just over two thirds of the dough and line the loaf tin. The remaining dough must be kept warm. Mix the cubed pork, herbs, lemon juice, water and seasoning. Place one third of the meat mixture in the base of the dough case and cover this with half of the raisins; repeat this operation once more then finish with the remaining meat mixture. Roll out the rest of the dough for the lid, brush the edge of the dough case and place on the lid; press edges well together.

Make a hole in the top. Decorate with dough leaves made from the scraps of dough. Brush with beaten egg. Place in the oven. Remove from the oven about 30 minutes before the end of the cooking period; leave to cool a little then remove from the loaf tin and quickly brush the sides of the pie with beaten egg. Replace in the oven and complete the cooking. Remove from the oven and cool on a wire rack.

Using a funnel pour aspic jelly through the hole in the top of the pie.

Serve with mustard and various pickles.

Note: This recipe was found at a farmhouse in the Midlands. The pork pies are always made with layers of stoned raisins between the layers of pork.

GALATINE OF VEAL

Approximately 3 hours

Scalded white tape and pudding cloth
Serves 6–8

INGREDIENTS

3 lb (1.35 kg) breast of veal—boned
1½ lb (675 g) sausage meat
8 oz (225 g) cooked ham—chopped
1 truffle—chopped
few gherkins—sliced
4 oz (100 g) pistachio nuts—skinned
1 clove garlic—juice
½ lemon—juice
½ pint (275 ml) aspic jelly

METHOD

Lay the breast of veal on a working surface; flatten and season. Spread half the sausage meat over the veal. Cover with the ham, truffle, gherkins and pistachio nuts then sprinkle over the garlic blended with the lemon juice. Spread the remaining sausage meat over then roll up the veal into a good shape and tie with the tape. Put into pudding cloth and place in a pan of boiling water. Boil for 5 minutes then simmer. After 3 hours remove from the heat and allow veal to cool in the liquid. When the veal is nearly cold remove from the liquid and take off the pudding cloth. Leave to set under a heavy weight in a cool place. Remove tape and coat veal with a layer of aspic jelly. When this layer of aspic jelly has set coat with another layer.

To serve place on a serving dish and cut off the first slice so that the pretty marbled effect made by the truffle and gerkins is shown.

SAUSAGE MEAT FOR GALATINE OF VEAL

INGREDIENTS

12 oz (350 g) lean pork
8 oz (225 g) pork fat
4 oz (100 g) lean veal
2 oz (50 g) fresh white breadcrumbs
¼ lemon—grated peel
⅓ small nutmeg—grated
½ teaspoon dried sage
½ teaspoon dried thyme
pinch dried marjoram
seasoning

METHOD

Mince the pork fat and veal and then mix all ingredients thoroughly together.

GREAT GRANDMOTHER'S ORANGE SALAD

Serves 5–6

INGREDIENTS

1 lb (450 g) oranges
1 tablespoon salad oil
2 tablespoons tarragon vinegar
1 tablespoon Madeira

METHOD

Skin and slice the oranges. Blend the oil, vinegar and madeira together. Arrange in a dish and pour over the dressing. This is best served well chilled.

WINTER SALAD NO. 1
Adapted from Mrs Beeton's *Book Of Household Management* (1902)

Serves 5–6

INGREDIENTS
1 endive
mustard and cress
1 beetroot—boiled
4 large hard boiled eggs
6 sticks celery

METHOD
Arrange the endive, mustard and cress high in the centre of a salad bowl or dish; garnish with sliced beetroot, eggs and shredded celery. These must be placed around the base of the endive mixture. Pour salad dressing over the garnishing.

SALAD DRESSING NO. 1

INGREDIENTS
3 tablespoons salad oil
1 teaspoon tarragon vinegar
1 teaspoon wine vinegar
seasoning

METHOD
Blend ingredients thoroughly together.

WINTER SALAD NO. 2
Adapted from Mrs Beeton's *Book of Household Management* (1911)

Serves 4–6

INGREDIENTS
1 small head celery
1 beetroot
3 potatoes—boiled
seasoning
1 teaspoon fresh parsley—finely chopped

METHOD
Slice the celery, beetroot and potatoes and arrange in separate layers in a large bowl. Season each layer. Pour over about four tablespoons of salad dressing then sprinkle on the parsley to garnish.

SALAD DRESSING NO. 2
Adapted from Mrs Beeton's *Book of Household Management* (1902)

INGREDIENTS
2 large eggs
1 teaspoon mustard powder
½ teaspoon salt
3 tablespoons salad oil
1½ tablespoons wine vinegar

METHOD
Hard boil the eggs. Take out the yolks and sieve, blending with the mustard powder and salt. Slowly add the oil stirring constantly, then add the vinegar drop by drop and stir to a cream.

GREAT GRANDMOTHER'S CHRISTMAS TRIFLE

4 pint (2 litre) trifle bowl
Serves 12

INGREDIENTS
for the base:

8 macaroons
3 tablespoons raspberry jam
40 ratafias
¼ pint (150 ml) sweet white wine
2 tablespoons sherry
1 lemon—juice and grated rind
4 slices pineapple, fresh or preserved

for the Vanilla Custard:

1 vanilla pod
1 pint (500 ml) milk
5 large egg yolks
4 tablespoons caster sugar
1 tablespoon cornflour

for the Topping:

1 pint (500 ml) double cream
curaçao to taste

Decorations for the top of the Trifle
Gold or silver covered almonds, crystallized rose petals and violets

METHOD

Put the macaroons in the base of trifle bowl then spread the raspberry jam over the macaroons. Add the ratafias then pour over the white wine mixed with the sherry and lemon. Cut each slice of pineapple into 8 wedges and cover the trifle base.

To make the custard put the vanilla pod and milk in a saucepan and bring to the boil. Remove from the heat and allow the vanilla pod to infuse in the milk for 30 minutes. Remove the vanilla pod and return the milk to a moderate heat. Whisk together the egg yolks, caster sugar and cornflour and add to the milk. Stir until the mixture thickens then remove from heat and allow to cool.

Pour the cooled custard over the other ingredients in the bowl. Whisk together the double cream and curaçao until thick and pour over the custard. Decorate.

CHOCOLATE CREAM

Serves 6–8

INGREDIENTS
8 oz (225 g) grated dessert chocolate
1 oz (25 g) caster sugar
2 tablespoons brandy
1½ pints (845 ml) double cream
toasted almonds—to garnish

METHOD
Place the grated chocolate in a bowl and pour over it as much hot water as will melt it. Add the sugar and beat with a balloon whisk until it becomes cold then whisk in the brandy. Whip the double cream then gradually whisk in the chocolate mixture.

Serve in individual glasses with toasted blanched almonds cut into thin strips sprinkled on the top.

BURNT CREAM

1¾ pint (1 litre) serving dish
Serves 6–8

INGREDIENTS

1 pint (570 ml) single cream
1 tablespoon caster sugar
1 stick cinnamon
1 lemon—grated rind
6 large eggs
2 tablespoons orange water
1 tablespoon cornflour
4 oz (100 g) demerara sugar

METHOD

Mix the cream, sugar, cinnamon and lemon rind in a large bowl then place the bowl over a pan of simmering water (do not let the bowl touch the water). When the cream mixture reaches boiling point remove from the heat. Place 6 egg yolks and 4 egg whites, the orange water and the cornflour in another large bowl and blend together; gradually pour the hot cream into the egg mixture stirring continually with a wooden spoon. Place the bowl containing the hot cream mixture over the pan of simmering water and stir until the mixture coats the back of the wooden spoon. Remove from the heat and pour into the serving dish. Leave until the cream is cold. When it is cold cover and leave in a cool place for a few hours (this cream is really best made the day before it is required).

About 3 hours before serving sprinkle the demerara sugar over the top of the cream and place under a hot grill then watch until it becomes golden. Chill again for about 2 to 3 hours before serving. The caramel should look like a glass plate on top of the cream.

GREAT GRANDMOTHER'S ROSE CREAMS

Serves 6–8

INGREDIENTS

1 oz (25 g) powdered gelatine
4 tablespoons rosewater
1 pint (425 ml) full cream milk
3 oz (75 g) sugar cubes
few drops pink food colouring
1 pint (425 ml) double cream—whipped until thick

METHOD

Mix together the powdered gelatine and rosewater in a small bowl and leave to soak. Pour the milk into a saucepan and add the sugar cubes. Place over a gentle heat and stir until the sugar has dissolved. Place the bowl containing the soaked gelatine over a saucepan of simmering water (do not let the bowl touch the water) and stir the gelatine with a metal spoon until dissolved. The spoon will be free of granules when this is achieved. Allow the gelatine to cool slightly Pour the warm milk mixture through a sieve into a large bowl then quickly pour and stir the transparent gelatine into it. Leave to cool and when lukewarm stir in the pink food colouring. Whip the cream until thick and fold into the milk mixture.

Pour into individual glasses and leave until set. Place a crystallized rose petal on the top of each cream to decorate.

DISH OF SNOW

Serves 10–12

INGREDIENTS

2½ lb (1.15 kg) cooking apples
2½ lb (1.15 kg) cox's orange pippen
1 lemon—grated rind
6 oz (175 g) caster sugar
12 large egg whites

METHOD

Peel, core and slice the apples and place them with the grated lemon rind in a large saucepan. Cover and leave on a very low heat until the apples soften. As soon as the apples are soft rub them through a sieve into a large bowl. Whisk the egg whites until stiff then gradually whisk in the caster sugar. Then whisk in the sieved apple mixture and continue whisking until the mixture looks as stiff as snow.

To serve turn the snow out onto a plain platter if possible and heap the snow up as high as you can. Garnish with sprigs of imitation holly around the base of the snow to give a real Christmas feel.

ORANGE FOOL

Serves 10–12

INGREDIENTS

6 seville oranges—juice only
6 large eggs—beaten
2 pints (850 ml) double cream
little grated nutmeg
½ teaspoon ground cinnamon
caster sugar—to taste

METHOD

Mix the juice of the oranges with the eggs, cream, nutmeg, cinnamon and sugar to taste. Place in a bowl over simmering water (do not let the bowl touch the water) and stir until it becomes as thick as melted butter. It must not be boiled. Then pour into a serving dish.

Serve cold.

ORANGE FRUIT SALAD
Adapted from Mrs Beeton's *Book Of Household Management* (1861)

Serves 5–6

INGREDIENTS
6 oranges
4 oz (100 g) muscatel raisins (stoned)
2 oz (50 g) caster sugar
4 tablespoons brandy
little ground cinnamon and ground cloves—optional

METHOD

Peel 5 of the oranges; divide them into slices without breaking the pulp and arrange them on a serving dish. Mix the raisins with the sugar and brandy and mingle them with the oranges. Squeeze the juice of the remaining orange over the salad. Add spices if required.

COMPÔTE OF ORANGES

Serves 12

INGREDIENTS
12 oranges
1 lb (450 g) caster sugar
¼ pint (150 ml) brandy or rum

METHOD
Pare off the rind of the oranges very thinly and reserve it. Divide the oranges into halves using a very sharp knife. Remove the white pithy cord which runs down the centre of the fruit and cut off all the pith. Pile the fruit up rather high on a dish. Put the rind kept in reserve into a saucepan with the sugar and 1 pint (570 ml) water and boil for 6 minutes; strain syrup into a jug and add the brandy or rum. Pour syrup mixture over the fruit.

Serve cold.

STEWED PEARS IN PORT WINE

Serves 4

INGREDIENTS
¼ pint (150 ml) water
½ pint (275 ml) port wine
2 oz (50 g) sugar cubes
1 strip lemon rind—pith removed
1 tablespoon red currant jelly
1" (2.5 cm) cinnamon stick
4 dessert pears
1 teaspoon arrowroot
2 oz (50 g) almonds—flaked and toasted

METHOD

Put the water, port wine, sugar cubes, strip of lemon rind, jelly and cinnamon in a saucepan over a gentle heat until the sugar has dissolved, then bring to the boil and boil for 1 minute. Peel, core and halve the pears lengthwise and add to the syrup. Cover the pan and simmer until the pears are tender. Remove the pears carefully and arrange them attractively on a serving dish. Strain the syrup through a sieve into a bowl; return syrup to the saucepan and place over a medium heat. Mix the arrowroot with a tablespoonful of water before adding to the syrup. Stir until boiling. Spoon the port wine sauce over the pears. Leave until cold then scatter over the toasted almond flakes.

SYLLABUB

Serves 12

INGREDIENTS
6 oz (175 g) sugar cubes
3 lemons
¾ pint (425 ml) sweet white wine
1½ pint (850 ml) double cream

METHOD

Rub the sugar cubes on the rinds of the lemons until soaked in the oil. Place the cubes in a bowl with the juice from the lemons and the white wine. Leave covered overnight. After standing slowly add the cream, stirring continually; when all the cream is incorporated whisk until the syllabub is thick enough to stand up in soft peaks. Pour into individual glasses and serve with ratafia biscuits.

Note: Keep in a cool place until required; do not refrigerate.

GREAT GRANDMOTHER'S COFFEE AND RUM CAKE

MODERATE OVEN
Gas Mark 4   350°F   180°C

Approximately 1–1¼ hours

7″ × 3″ (18 × 7.5 cm) non-stick round cake tin—lightly buttered base lined with greaseproof paper

INGREDIENTS

6 oz (175 g) soft butter
6 oz (175 g) caster sugar
3 large eggs
7 oz (200 g) self-raising flour
1 oz (25 g) cornflour
pinch salt
1 tablespoon hot rum

for the Rum Syrup:

¼ pint (150 ml) water—minus 1 tablespoon
1 tablespoon Camp Coffee
4 oz (100 g) caster sugar
3 tablespoons rum

for the Topping:

4 oz (100 g) icing sugar—sifted
¼ pint (150 ml) double cream
6 tablespoons rum
2 oz (50 g) roasted almond nibs

METHOD

Warm the caster sugar for no more than a few seconds in the oven. Cream butter and sugar until light and fluffy then whisk in the first egg. As soon as this is incorporated whisk in the second and then the third egg. Sift together the flour, cornflour and salt. Using a balloon whisk gradually fold the flour mixture into the creamed butter and sugar and then quickly fold in the rum. Pour into prepared cake tin, smooth over the top then make a slight hollow in the centre. This helps to give a flat surface to the finished cake. Place in the oven and cook until golden and firm to the touch. Turn cake out onto a wire rack and leave to cool. Remove greaseproof paper.

For the syrup boil the water, coffee and sugar for 5 minutes and then remove from the heat and add the rum. Place the cake on a cake stand or plate and pour syrup over the cake and leave for 12 hours.

Gradually whisk the sifted icing sugar into the double cream for the topping. Still whisking add the rum a tablespoonful at a time. Then whisk until the mixture forms soft peaks. Spread the mixture over the top of the cake and sprinkle on the roasted nuts.

GREAT GRANDMOTHER'S CURAÇAO SPONGE ROLL

FAIRLY HOT OVEN
Gas Mark 5   375°F 190°C

Approximately 12 minutes

Genoese tin 14¾″ × 11″ (38 × 28 cm) or Swiss roll tray lightly buttered and lined with non-stick pure baking parchment

INGREDIENTS

3 large eggs
4 oz (100 g) caster sugar
1 teaspoon orange water
½ lemon—grated rind and juice
3 oz (75 g) plain flour
1 oz (25 g) cornflour
1½ teaspoons baking powder
pinch salt
1 tablespoon hot butter

for the Curaçao Butter Cream:

8 oz (225 g) soft butter
9 oz (250 g) icing sugar—sifted
4 tablespoons curaçao

METHOD

PRE-HEAT OVEN

Sift together the flour, cornflour, baking powder and salt. Separate the eggs. Whisk egg whites until firm, then whisk in 2 tablespoons of the caster sugar. When stiff fold in 1 tablespoon of caster sugar with a balloon whisk. Put the egg yolks, orange water, remaining sugar, grated lemon rind and juice into a warmed bowl and whisk until thick. Fold into the egg yolk mixture 2 tablespoons of the whisked egg white mixture, then fold in the remaining egg white mixture. Fold in the sifted flour. Quickly fold in the hot butter. Pour onto prepared tray, spread mixture evenly but gently over the base. Place in the oven and cook until firm to the touch and a light golden colour.

Turn sponge out onto a clean damp cloth wrung out in cold water. Remove the paper. Place a fresh sheet of greaseproof paper over the sponge. Now taking the cloth in one hand roll up the sponge so that the greaseproof paper is on the inside of the sponge roll. Leave to cool.

To make the butter cream. Whisk the butter until light and fluffy. Gradually add the icing sugar and then the curaçao.

To serve unroll the sponge and remove the greaseproof paper. Spread the butter cream over the sponge and roll it up again. Dust the roll very thickly with sifted icing sugar. Pour 4 tablespoons of curaçao onto the serving plate and carefully place on the sponge roll.

WHIM WHAM

Serves 6

INGREDIENTS
1 pint (570 ml) double cream
1 glass sherry
1 lemon—grated rind
2 oz (50 g) caster sugar
12 savoy biscuits
8 oz (225 g) red currant jelly
1 oz (25 g) candied lemon peel—chopped

METHOD
Whisk the cream with the sherry, lemon rind and sugar. Cut the biscuits through and cover the base of a serving dish with half of them; spread one third of the cream over the biscuits and then put little heaps of red currant jelly over the cream using half of the jelly. Repeat this once more; finishing with a layer of cream. Sprinkle the chopped peel over the top.

TIPSY CAKE

Otherwise known as trifle. The sponge cake recipe for this dish appears on page 138. Please note that the preparations for this dish take 4 days.

Serves 10–12

INGREDIENTS
1 sponge cake—about 3 days old
jam—to choice
2 fl oz (60 ml) brandy
2 fl oz (60 ml) white wine
8 oz (225 g) almonds—blanched, skinned and cut into strips
1½ pints (700 ml) almond custard

METHOD
Make the sponge cake according to the instructions on page 138. Slice the sponge in half then sandwich the 2 halves together with chosen jam. Place the sponge in a large glass bowl then pierce several times with a skewer. Mix the brandy with the white wine and pour over the sponge. Place the almond strips in lines on the top. Cover and leave to soak for 24 hours.

ALMOND CUSTARD

Makes about 1½ pints (845 ml)

INGREDIENTS
3 oz (75 g) cornflour
1 pint (425 ml) milk
½ pint (275 ml) single cream
9 large egg yolks
6 oz (150 g) caster sugar
1 oz (25 g) melted butter
1 tablespoon amaretto

METHOD

Combine the milk and single cream. Blend the cornflour in a large bowl with a little of the milk mixture, then beat in the egg yolks and caster sugar. Heat the remaining milk mixture in a large heavy based saucepan until hot but not boiling. Remove from the heat then gradually pour the hot milk mixture onto the cornflour mixture stirring continuously. Return blended mixture to the saucepan and stir over a medium heat until the mixture thickens; then stir in the melted butter. Remove from the heat and stir in the amaretto. Leave the custard to cool a little then pour over soaked sponge. Cover and chill for about 1½ hours.

VICTORIAN COFFEE MERINGUE

SLOW OVEN
Gas Mark 1   275°F 140°C

Approximately 1 hour

Cut out 2 circles 8″ (20 cm) diameter of non-stick pure parchment baking paper and place on baking trays

INGREDIENTS

for the Meringue:

6 oz (175 g) caster sugar
3 standard egg whites
2 oz (50 g) assorted nuts—chopped finely

for the Filling:

3 standard egg yolks
3 oz (75 g) caster sugar
2 teaspoons powdered gelatine
4 teaspoons Camp coffee essence
¼ pint (150 ml) double cream—lightly whipped
3 tablespoons preserved ginger—sliced

METHOD

Place the egg whites in a large bowl and whisk until stiff. Add half of the sugar and continue whisking until stiff again. Carefully fold in the remaining sugar and the chopped nuts. Spoon half of the meringue mixture onto each piece of baking parchment and spread the mixture out evenly to cover the rounds. Place in the oven and cook until firm and crisp throughout. Remove and leave until completely cold.

To make the filling put the egg yolks and sugar into a large bowl. Then place the bowl over a saucepan of simmering water, but do not allow the bowl to touch the water. Whisk the egg mixture until smooth and creamy. Remove from the heat and allow to cool. Stand a bowl containing 3 tablespoons of hot water over another saucepan of simmering water (do not let the bowl touch the water) then sprinkle in the gelatine powder and stir until dissolved. The spoon will be free of granules when this is completed. Blend the coffee essence into the cooled egg mixture, fold in the dissolved gelatine. Lightly whip the cream and fold into the mixture. Cover and chill for about 20 minutes or until the mixture has partially set and is firm enough for spreading.

To assemble place one round of meringue on a cake plate or stand. Spread the coffee cream over the top of the meringue then spoon on the sliced ginger. Cover with the remaining meringue.

To decorate place ¼ pint (150 ml) whipped double cream into a piping bag fitted with a large rose nozzle and swirl around the top edge of the meringue. Place extra slices of preserved ginger in the cream.

Note: The authors wish to express their thanks to the manufacturers of Camp Coffee for supplying this recipe.

THE HIDDEN MOUNTAIN
Adapted from Mrs Beeton's *Book Of Household Management* (1861)

Serves 3–4

INGREDIENTS
6 large eggs
½ large lemon
¼ pint (150 ml) single cream
sugar to taste
1 oz (25 g) butter
jam—to choice
reserved lemon slices
frosted holly leaves—see recipe page 163

METHOD
Skin the lemon and remove the pith. Slice the fruit into paper thin segments. Reserve 5 slices to garnish. Separate the eggs and beat the whites and yolks individually. Then combine and beat again. Add a few slices of the lemon, the cream and sufficient sugar to sweeten. Heat the butter in a large omelette pan and then pour in the mixture and fry as a pancake, but note that it should be 3 times the size of an ordinary pancake. Slide out onto a serving plate then cover the surface with a layer of jam. Leave until cool then garnish with slices of lemon and 1 or 2 frosted holly leaves. Serve cold.

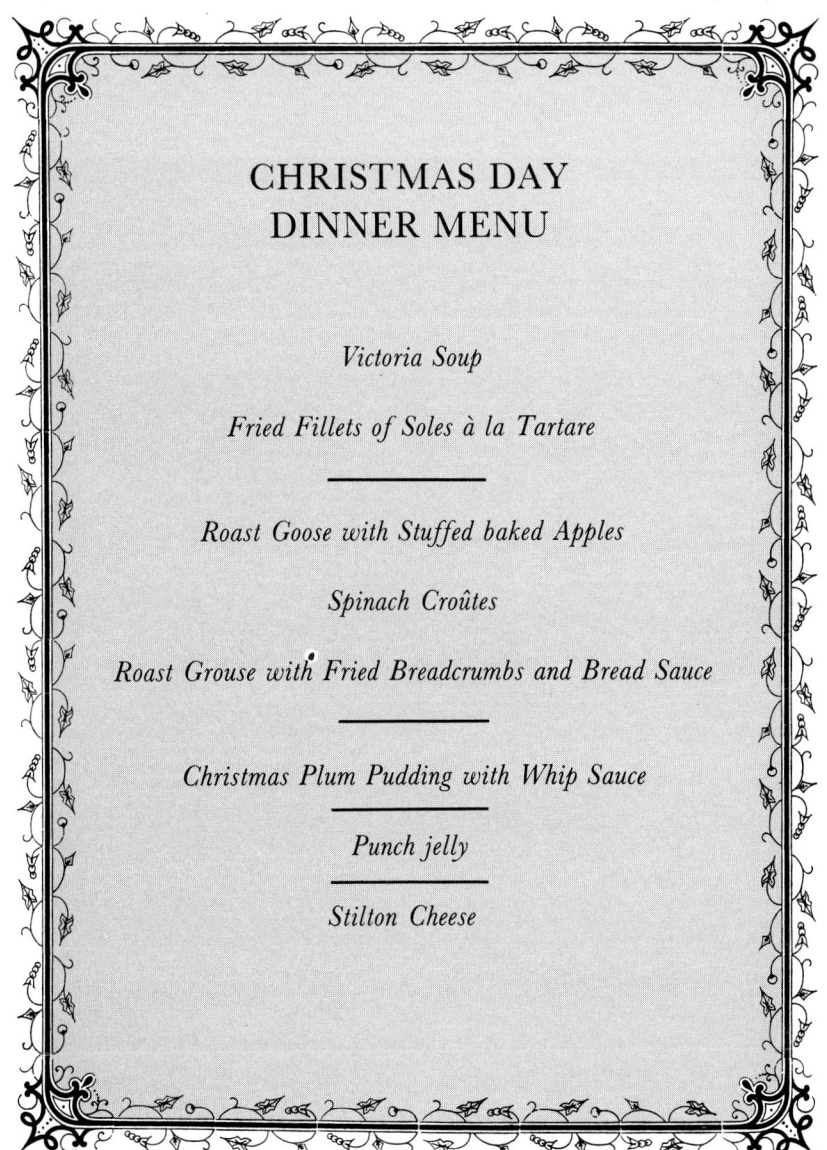

CHRISTMAS DAY
DINNER MENU

Victoria Soup

Fried Fillets of Soles à la Tartare

———————

Roast Goose with Stuffed baked Apples

Spinach Croûtes

Roast Grouse with Fried Breadcrumbs and Bread Sauce

———————

Christmas Plum Pudding with Whip Sauce

———————

Punch jelly

———————

Stilton Cheese

Christmas comes, but too soon is on its way,
so lets be happy while we may

Try to create a festive Victorian atmosphere by perhaps suggesting
to your guests that they bring an outfit of the period.
Complete the scene by using evergreen garlands, as a form of decoration,
covered at the high points by large satin bows and if possible
dress the Christmas tree with home made decorations.
The festive table setting should include a Christmas cracker at each place setting
and a matching napkin ring looks attractive. Arrange small dishes
piled high with sweetmeats, fresh fruits, mixed nuts,
blanched almonds and raisins down the centre of the table with
a festive table centrepiece. The glow of candle light will add
the finishing touch to the traditional scene you have created

After your Victorian feast, games, carol singing,
dancing or other diversions can provide
a great deal of additional pleasure and amusement.

Our Christmas Day Dinner has been designed to serve 12 people. To ease serving a hostess trolley and large heated tray are really necessary to keep the various courses hot until required.

From our own experience we know how important it is to know in what order the different dishes should be prepared. Here then is a proposed running schedule for the entire meal.

Make up and cook the recipe for the Sage and Onion Stuffing and leave to cool. Prepare the goose for roasting and place in the pre-heated oven.

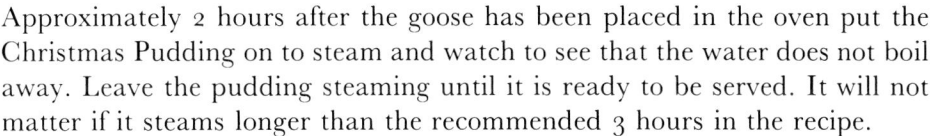

Approximately 2 hours after the goose has been placed in the oven put the Christmas Pudding on to steam and watch to see that the water does not boil away. Leave the pudding steaming until it is ready to be served. It will not matter if it steams longer than the recommended 3 hours in the recipe.

Prepare the grouse for roasting while the goose is cooking. Leave in a cool place loosely covered with foil until they are due to be placed in the overn.

Approximately 1 hour before the goose is ready to be removed from the oven prepare and start to cook the Victoria Soup. Once the soup is simmering refer to the recipe for the sauce for the goose and start making the stock.

Prepare the Stuffed Apples according to the instructions and place in the oven for the last 30 minutes roasting time. When the goose is done remove and place on a serving dish to keep warm along with the apples. At this point the grouse can be put in the oven.

Drain the goose fat from the roasting tin and leave to cool. Then cover and store in a cool place. The remaining juices in the tin can then be used to complete the sauce for the goose.

At this point you should be ready to sieve the Victoria Soup, add the milk and keep warm until required. The roast grouse should be ready to remove from the oven and put to warm with the goose.

You can now start making the bread sauce recipe and cook the fillets for the Fried Fillets of Sole. Keep both dishes warm. Now fry the breadcrumbs.

Finally cook the spinach for the Spinach Croûtes and leave to drain in a sieve placed over a bowl. When the moment arrives to serve the Croûtes start the recipe as it only takes a few minutes and is best served fresh.

The Whip Sauce for the Christmas Pudding can be left to stand for about 30 minutes covered in a cool place. Don't worry if it starts to liquify at the bottom of the bowl it can be brought back to its original consistency by replacing the bowl over hot water and whisking the contents again.

You should now be ready to call the guests to dinner.

VICTORIA SOUP

Adapted from *A Year's Cookery* by Phyllis Browne (1898)

Serves 12

INGREDIENTS

1 oz (25 g) clarified butter
1 large onion
1 large carrot
2 sticks celery
3 pints (1.7 litres) chicken stock
1 bay leaf
1 sprig fresh parsley
½ teaspoon dried thyme
3 oz (75 g) rice—washed
seasoning to taste
½ pint (275 ml) milk
½ pint (275 ml) single cream

METHOD

Slice the carrot, onion and celery. Heat the butter in a large saucepan, then put in the onion and sauté until golden. Add the celery and carrot and cook for a further 5 minutes. Add the chicken stock, bay leaf, parsley, thyme and rice. Bring to the boil, reduce heat and simmer covered for about 1½ hours or until the rice is soft. Remove bay leaf and parsley. Place a fine sieve over a clean pan and pour the liquid through the sieve. Rub the vegetables and rice through the sieve. Add the milk and cream, season to taste and warm through again. Keep warm until required for serving.

Note: The chicken stock can be made and frozen up to 3 months beforehand or made the day it is required and placed in a covered container in the refrigerator.

FRIED FILLETS OF SOLE
A LA TARTARE

Serves 12

INGREDIENTS
12 small skinned fillets of sole
seasoned flour
2 large eggs—beaten
white breadcrumbs
oil or clarified butter—or mixture of the two
Tartare sauce
1 lemon—finely sliced

METHOD

Wash and dry fillets, coat with seasoned flour then dip in beaten eggs and finally coat with breadcrumbs. Lay each breadcrumbed fillet on a plate covered with breadcrumbs until all fillets are ready for frying.

When all of the fillets are breadcrumbed, heat the oil and or clarified butter to 350°F. Carefully lower each fillet into the hot fat and fry until golden.

Drain on absorbent white kitchen paper towels and keep warm.

To serve place a fillet in the centre of each plate; spoon a little tartare sauce on top of the fillet. Garnish with a slice of lemon.

Note: Breadcrumbs can be previously prepared. Remove the crust from a large stale white or brown loaf and rub through a wire sieve or use an electric food processor. Spread the crumbs out onto a tray and cover with a sheet of greaseproof paper (to keep off dust). Leave for two days in a warm place. Store in an airtight container and use as required.

TARTARE SAUCE

Adapted from *Cassell's New Universal Cookery Book* by Lizzie Heritage (1896)

Makes approximately ¾ pint (425 ml)

INGREDIENTS

2 large egg yolks
1 teaspoon salt
ground white pepper
½ pint (275 ml) olive oil
1 teaspoon white wine vinegar
¼ teaspoon lemon juice
¼ teaspoon lemon rind—grated
pinch cayenne pepper
1 teaspoon Worcester sauce
1 teaspoon mushroom ketchup
¼ teaspoon french mustard
2 tablespoons double cream

METHOD

Put egg yolks into a large bowl, then add the salt and pepper; mix well together. Add one drop of oil and whisk in thoroughly. It is important that throughout the making of this mayonnaise you never stop whisking. Now add the oil a drop at a time until the mixture begins to thicken. When this happens but not before, add the oil in larger drops. Having used half of the oil, add the vinegar, this will thin the mixture down. Whisk in the rest of the oil in a thin steady trickle. You will now have a thick mayonnaise. Blend together the remaining ingredients and stir into the mayonnaise.

Note: Sauces that contain eggs can curdle if oil is added too fast. If this should happen break a fresh egg yolk into a bowl and whisk in the curdled mixture a drop at a time.

This tartare sauce, the basis of which is Mayonnaise, will keep for up to one week if put in the bottom of a refrigerator in a screw top jar.

ROAST GOOSE WITH STUFFED BAKED APPLES

FAIRLY HOT OVEN
Gas Mark 6   400°F 200°C

A young goose with yellow pliable feet should be chosen for roasting

Approximately 15 minutes per pound (450 g) plus 15 minutes over

Serves 12

INGREDIENTS
12 lb (5.4 kg) goose—dressed weight
sage and onion stuffing
seasoning
flour

METHOD
PRE-HEAT OVEN

Wipe the bird inside and out with a clean damp cloth. Remove fat from the cavity and use to bard the bird. Put the sage and onion stuffing into the cavity then truss the bird with clean white string. Place the bird on a rack in a roasting tin. Prick the skin all over with a fork. Season well then bard the bird with fat taken from the cavity. Cover bird loosely with cooking foil and place in the oven. Baste at 20 minute intervals. Drain the surplus fat from the roasting tin as it collects. After 1 hour remove the trussing. 30 minutes before the end of approximate roasting time remove the foil and dust the bird with flour. Place the stuffed apples in the oven see recipe pp. 78.

Test to see if the bird is cooked by piercing with a skewer in the thickest part of the leg. If the juices run clear the bird is cooked, if not cook on. Keep warm until required.

To serve place a slice of roast goose with stuffing and a stuffed baked apple on each plate. Pour a little sauce over the slice of goose.

SAGE AND ONION STUFFING FOR ROAST GOOSE
Adapted from the *Cook's Guide* by Charles Elmé Francatelli (1888)

INGREDIENTS
4 large onions
1 tablespoon dried sage
6 oz (175 g) fresh breadcrumbs
2 oz (50 g) butter
seasoning

METHOD
Chop the onions and parboil for two minutes; drain them through a sieve and afterwards put them in a saucepan with the sage, breadcrumbs, butter and seasoning. Place the saucepan over a low heat for twenty minutes stirring the stuffing occasionally. Leave to cool.

STUFFED BAKED APPLES FOR ROAST GOOSE

FAIRLY HOT OVEN
Gas Mark 6   400°F 200°C

Approximately 30 minutes

Serves 12

INGREDIENTS
12 cooking apples
1 oz (25 g) butter
1 medium onion—chopped
3 oz (75 g) dried apricots—soaked
1 oz (25 g) raisins—very finely chopped
2 oz (50 g) chopped walnuts
2 tablespoons curaçao

METHOD

Finely chop the apricots, raisins and onions. Remove the cores from the cooking apples then using a sharp knife make a cut in the skin around the middle of each apple and place in a baking dish. Heat the butter in a saucepan and soften the onion in it. Remove from the heat and add the remaining ingredients; mix thoroughly. Press the mixture into the cavity of each apple. Place in the oven with the bird for approximately the last 30 minutes of roasting time. Keep warm until required.

SAUCE FOR ROAST GOOSE

INGREDIENTS

a little goose fat
1 medium onion
giblets
1¼ pints (720 ml) dry cider
seasoning
juice from roasting tin
cornflour
1 orange—juice and grated rind
3 tablespoons red currant jelly
pinch mixed spice

METHOD

Finely chop the onion. Heat a little goose fat in a saucepan and soften the onion in it. Add the giblets, cider and seasoning then simmer for 1 hour. Remove from the heat and strain through a sieve into a jug. Drain the fat from the roasting tin and place the juices from the tin in a saucepan over a low heat. Thicken with cornflour. Stir constantly making sure the sauce is smooth and very gradually add the orange juice and rind, red currant jelly, spice and giblet stock. Keep warm until required.

SPINACH CROÛTES

Serves 12

INGREDIENTS

½ oz (10 g) butter
½ oz (10 g) plain flour
2 fl oz (50 g) single cream
1 pint (570 ml) spinach purée
seasoning
12 × 2½" (6 cm) squares of hot buttered toast

METHOD

Melt the butter in a saucepan over a low heat and make a roux by stirring in the flour; still stirring cook for 3 minutes. Add the cream to the roux and stir until blended then stir in the spinach purée. Season and heat through.

Serve a portion of the spinach on top of each square of buttered toast. This spinach has a delicate taste and is delicious.

FRIED BREADCRUMBS

INGREDIENTS

8 oz (225 g) fresh white breadcrumbs
12 oz (350 g) clarified butter

METHOD

Heat butter in a frying pan then toss in the breadcrumbs; stir until golden. Drain on kitchen paper towels. Keep warm.

ROAST GROUSE

Young grouse with pliable feet and a supple breastbone should be chosen for roasting. The grouse should be hung until the feathers pull out easily above the tail. It is sometimes possible to buy an oven ready frozen grouse. Please read the instructions on the wrapper very carefully before defrosting.

FAIRLY HOT OVEN
Gas Mark 6   400°F 200°C

Approximately 35–45 minutes

INGREDIENTS
6 grouse
ground black pepper
6 oz (160 g) soft butter
6 strips bacon fat
3 fl oz (90 ml) dry white wine
flour for dusting

METHOD
PRE-HEAT OVEN

Wipe the birds inside and out with a clean damp cloth. Blend together butter and pepper. Put a portion of the butter mixture into the cavity of each bird. Pour the wine into the roasting tin. Truss the birds; place well apart in the roasting tin (do not let the birds touch one another) and lay over them the strips of bacon fat. Baste frequently. Remove strips of bacon fat for the last 10 minutes of roasting time and dust the birds lightly with flour; roast until the juices run clear when thighs are pierced with a skewer. Remove the trussing. Keep warm until required.

To serve cut each grouse in half lengthways and place cavity side down on each plate. Serve with a few fried breadcrumbs and a little bread sauce.

Note: There are several species of grouse. Red grouse are found in the mountain districts in the North of England and Scotland. Other species are the black grouse—also called the "grey hen" and the Cock of the Wood better known as "Capercaillie".

BREAD SAUCE

Makes approximately 1 pint (500 ml)

INGREDIENTS
4 oz (100 g) fresh white breadcrumbs
½ pint (300 ml) milk
1 clove garlic
1 small onion
1 bay leaf
3 cloves
1 oz (25 g) butter
seasoning
8 fl oz (225 ml) single cream

METHOD
Finely chop the onion. Put the breadcrumbs into a saucepan with the milk, garlic juice, onion, bay leaf, cloves, butter and seasoning. Bring slowly to the boil, remove from the heat and leave to infuse for 30 minutes. Remove the bay leaf and cloves. Gently reheat while stirring in the cream and heat through. Keep warm until required.

GREAT GRANDMOTHER'S CHRISTMAS PLUM PUDDING

One 4 lb (2 kg) and one 2 lb (1 kg) basin or three 2 lb (1 kg) basins—buttered
buttered greaseproof paper and cooking foil

Steam for 9 hours then for a further 3 hrs on Christmas Day

INGREDIENTS

8 oz (225 g) grated suet
10 oz (275 g) fresh white breadcrumbs
8 oz (225 g) self-raising flour
12 oz (350 g) sultanas
12 oz (350 g) muscatel raisins
1 lb (450 g) currants
2 oz (50 g) candied citron peel
4 oz (100 g) candied lemon peel
4 oz (100 g) candied orange peel
3 oz (75 g) almonds—blanched, skinned
1 lb (450 g) demerara sugar
1 lemon—grated rind and juice
1 orange—grated rind
1 teaspoon grated nutmeg
1½ teaspoons ground cloves
1 tablespoon ground cinnamon
6 large eggs
¾ pint (425 ml) stout
3 tablespoons brandy
3 tablespoons rum

METHOD

Thinly slice the candied peel and almonds. Blend the stout, brandy and rum. Place all the ingredients in a large bowl and mix thoroughly, the mixture should be of a soft dropping consistency. Cover and leave in the mixing bowl overnight.

Put mixture into prepared basins and fill to about 1″ (2.5 cm) from the top. Cover each basin with buttered greaseproof paper which in turn is to be covered with cooking foil; tie on to the basin with string under the rim and make a loop over the top to form a handle. Steam for 9 hours. Watch to see that the water does not boil away.

Leave to cool then replace the greaseproof paper and cooking foil with fresh. Store in a cool dry place. Steam for a further 3 hours before serving on Christmas Day.

To serve place pudding onto a serving plate and put a sprig of holly on the top. Cover in warmed brandy and ignite. The pudding, whilst still flaming, can be carried into the guests. Serve with Whip Sauce.

Note: An old English tradition when mixing the plum pudding is that each member of the family should have a stir for good luck. Another tradition is to add silver charms during mixing. Guests are told of the hidden treasure (and warned to be careful). It is considered very lucky if one is found in your piece of pudding. Harrods of Knightsbridge stock these charms.
    Make as far in advance as possible as they do improve with keeping.

WHIP SAUCE
Makes 2½ pints (1.4 L)

INGREDIENTS
6 large egg yolks
2 oz (50 g) caster sugar
¼ pint (150 ml) sherry
¼ lemon—grated rind and juice

METHOD
Put all the ingredients into a large bowl. Place bowl over a pan of simmering water (do not let the bowl touch the water). Whisk until it presents the appearance of a well-set creamy froth this takes about 7 minutes if using an electric hand whisk. When the sauce is made it can stand for about 30 minutes covered in a cool place. If the base of the sauce starts to liquify replace the bowl over hot water and whisk again. This can also be done to revive any leftover sauce which has been kept in the refrigerator.

Note: this sauce is also the perfect accompaniment for strawberries or other summer fruits.

PUNCH JELLY

Serves 12

INGREDIENTS

8 oz (225 g) fast dissolving sugar cubes
3 lemons
1 orange
1 pint (570 ml) boiling water
5 cloves
little grated nutmeg
½ stick cinnamon—bruised
¼ pint (150 ml) rum
¼ pint (150 ml) brandy
¼ pint (150 ml) lemon juice
3 tablespoons orange juice
1 oz (25 g) powdered gelatine

METHOD

Rub the sugar cubes over the lemon and orange rinds until the cubes are soaked with the zest.

Pour a pint of boiling water into a saucepan, add sugar, cloves, nutmeg and cinnamon. Place over a gentle heat and simmer for 10 minutes. Add the rum, brandy and fruit juices to the pan; gently heat all together.

Strain spiced liquid through a piece of muslin which has been placed over a sieve resting on a bowl. Stand the bowl with the spiced liquid in it over a saucepan of simmering water (do not let the bowl touch the water). Sprinkle on the powdered gelatine and stir with a metal spoon until dissolved. The spoon will be free of granules when this operation is completed.

To serve pour if possible into punch cups. If these are not available use small glasses; leave to set. This can be made the day before serving.

Note: Punch jelly does pack a punch so only a small portion is suggested. A frosted mint leaf looks attractive as a garnish (see pp. 163).

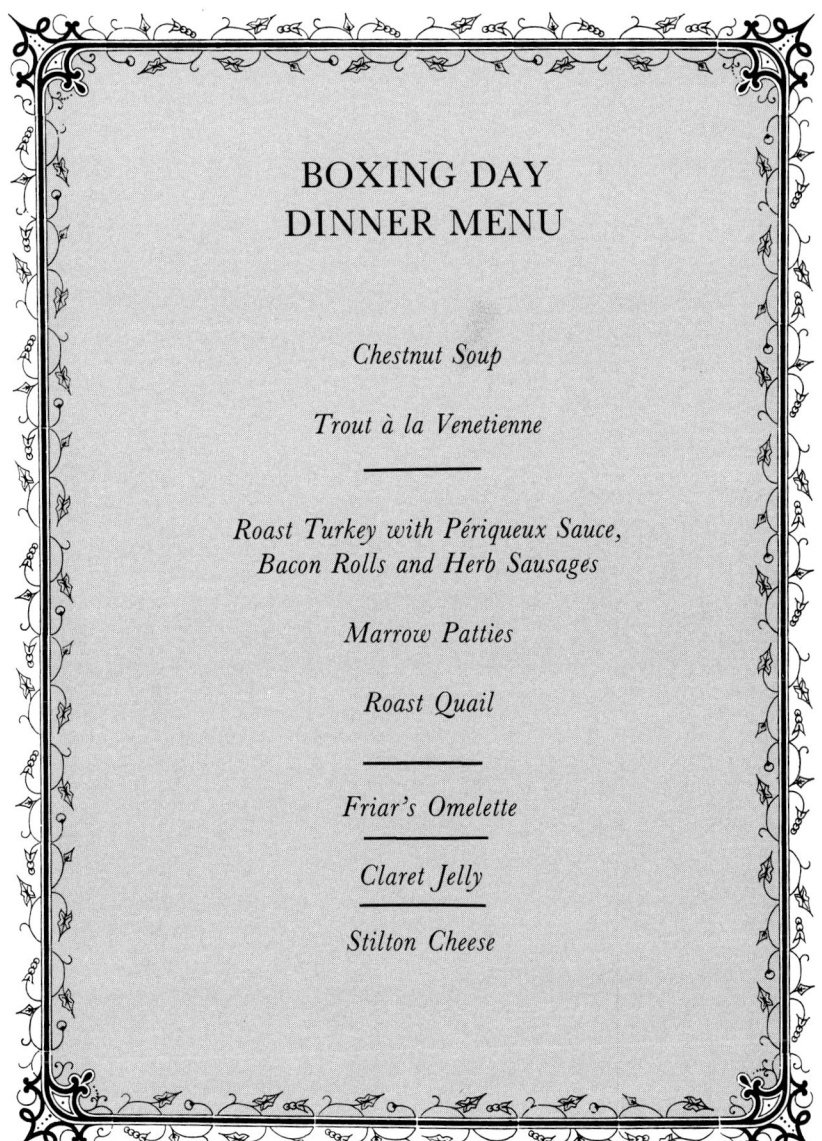

BOXING DAY
DINNER MENU

Chestnut Soup

Trout à la Venetienne

———

Roast Turkey with Périqueux Sauce,
Bacon Rolls and Herb Sausages

Marrow Patties

Roast Quail

———

Friar's Omelette

———

Claret Jelly

———

Stilton Cheese

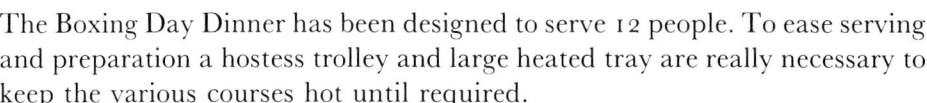

The Boxing Day Dinner has been designed to serve 12 people. To ease serving and preparation a hostess trolley and large heated tray are really necessary to keep the various courses hot until required.

Here is our proposed schedule for the entire meal. Do note that the Marrow Patties and Herb Sausages can be made the day before.

Make the forcemeat for the turkey and leave to cool. Prepare the turkey for roasting and place in the pre-heated oven.

Start the Chestnut Soup approximately 45 minutes before the turkey has finished cooking. Then prepare the quail for roasting and leave in a cool place loosely covered with foil until they are due to be placed in the oven. Now prepare the Trout à la Venetienne.

Remove the turkey from the oven once it is done and increase the oven temperature in order to roast the quail. Place the turkey on a serving dish and keep warm. Pour the turkey fat and juices into a container and place in the refrigerator.

When the oven has reached the right temperature for the quail remove their covering and place in the oven. Now fry the trout and when cooked keep warm. When the quail is roasted remove from the oven and keep the birds warm.

At this point remove the Herb Sausages and Marrow Patties from the refrigerator, complete the recipe instructions and cook. As they are cooking complete the Chestnut soup and then put all the dishes to warm.

Reduce the oven temperature for the Friars Omelette. Prepare and bake according to the instructions. Then prepare and grill the Bacon Rolls. You can now make the Orange Sauce for the trout and put to one side to keep warm.

Once the Friars Omelette is ready remove from the oven and leave to stand in the cake tin for 7 minutes. Then turn out onto a serving platter and cover loosely with foil—keep warm on a heated tray not inside a trolley as the breadcrumbs will harden. When it is ready to serve coat with icing sugar and decorate. It is just as delicious cold.

Just before sitting down to eat make the Périqueux sauce. Toast the rounds of bread for the Roast Quail and you should be perfectly prepared to serve your guests.

CHESTNUT SOUP

Serves 12

INGREDIENTS

1½ lb (700 g) chestnuts—shelled
sufficient beef stock to cover skinned chestnuts
4 pints (2.25 L) beef stock
salt
cayenne pepper
powdered mace
½ pint (275 ml) double cream

METHOD

Place the chestnuts in a large pan of warm water and bring to the boil. Remove from heat then lift out one chestnut at a time, quickly remove the brown skin and immerse in cold water. When all the peeling is completed drain off the cold water. Now cover the prepared chestnuts with beef stock and simmer them for about 45 minutes or until they break when pierced with a fork; then drain and rub through a fine sieve into a large saucepan. Add the stock, salt, cayenne and mace to taste. Place the saucepan over a medium heat and stir the ingredients often until boiling point is reached. Stir in the cream and keep hot until required.

Note: If no beef stock is available tinned consommé can be used.

TROUT A LA VENETIENNE

Adapted from *Warne's Model Cookery And Housekeeping Book*
compiled and edited by Mary Jewry (c. 1880)

INGREDIENTS

12 × 6 oz (175 g) trout
6 oz (175 g) soft butter
2 tablespoons fresh parsley—finely chopped
1 teaspoon dried chives
salad oil
fine breadcrumbs
clarified butter/oil—for frying

METHOD

Blend together the butter, chopped parsley and chives. Clean the trout, then make two parallel 1″ (2.5 cm) incisions on either side of each trout. Insert the butter mixture into the incisions. Place the trout in a large dish and pour a little salad oil over them. Leave for 30 minutes. Remove trout and coat with fine breadcrumbs. Fry over a moderate heat in the clarified butter/oil for about 5 minutes on each side. Drain on paper kitchen towels. Keep warm until required.

ORANGE SAUCE

INGREDIENTS

8 oranges
2 lemons
1½ tablespoons arrowroot

METHOD

Blend together the juice of all the oranges and lemons plus the grated rind of 1 orange. Put the orange mixture into a saucepan over a moderate heat and stir constantly until it thickens.

Serve each trout coated with orange sauce.

ROAST TURKEY WITH PERIGUEUX SAUCE

Choose a turkey with a plump, firm breast and bright, bulging eyes for roasting.

If buying a frozen turkey always read the instructions on the wrapper very carefully before defrosting. This is very important.

HOT OVEN
Gas Mark 5   375°F   190°C

Approximately 20 minutes per pound (450 g) plus 20 minutes over

INGREDIENTS
11 lb (5kg) turkey—dressed weight
12 oz (350 g) soft butter
seasoning
1 medium onion—quartered
forcemeat

METHOD
PRE-HEAT OVEN

Wipe the bird inside and out with a clean damp cloth. Gently loosen skin over the breast of the bird by lifting up the skin at the neck end and with your hand underneath the skin gradually and gently ease the skin away from the flesh. Be very careful, the skin must not be torn. Place forcemeat well into the cavity. When the forcemeat has been inserted, pull the skin down loosely over the back of the neck (to allow for the expansion of the forcemeat) and secure with a skewer or sew up with scalded white thread. Gently pat the breast back into a nice shape. Season the cavity and place in the quartered onion. Truss the bird and place in a roasting tin. Spread the soft butter over the top of the bird then cover loosely with cooking foil. Baste at 20 minute intervals. After 1 hour remove the trussing. 30 minutes before the end of the roasting period remove the foil in order to let the bird brown.

Test to see if the bird is cooked by piercing the thickest part of the leg with a skewer. There should be no sign of any pink juice. If this is the case then continue roasting until the juice runs out clear and golden. Remove from the oven. Place turkey on a serving plate and keep warm.

FORCEMEAT FOR TURKEY

INGREDIENTS

1 medium onion
1 oz (25 g) butter
6 oz (150 g) minced bacon
4 oz (100 g) cooking apples
4 oz (100 g) fresh breadcrumbs
1 tablespoon dried sage
¼ lemon—juice and grated rind
1 large egg
seasoning

METHOD

Core, peel and finely chop the apples. Chop the onions and fry in the butter until golden. Remove from the heat and add the remaining ingredients; mix together thoroughly. Leave to cool.

PERIGUEUX SAUCE

INGREDIENTS

1 oz (25 g) butter
2 tablespoons flour
2 tablespoons tomato purée
1 pint (570 ml) beef stock—see recipe pp.112
½ pint (275 ml) Madeira
1½ tablespoons beef glaze—see recipe pp.113
nut of butter
12 oz (350 g) tin of truffles in juice

METHOD

Put butter and flour into a saucepan and cook slowly to a brown roux, stirring constantly. Stir in the tomato purée and very gradually add the stock making sure that the mixture remains smooth. Simmer and stir for 5 minutes.

Place the madeira and glaze in a saucepan. Blend then reduce to half the quantity over a medium heat. Add the blended stock and simmer for 3 minutes. Remove from the heat and stir in the nut of butter a little at a time then add the finely chopped truffle and juice. Keep warm until required.

Note: If no beef stock or glaze is available substitute undiluted concentrated tinned consommé. To obtain the amount of glaze required for the sauce reduce a 10 oz (295 g) tin of concentrated consommé in a small saucepan and follow the instructions for the beef stock and glaze recipe on pp.112.

GRILLED BACON ROLLS

INGREDIENTS

12 rashers bacon—rinds removed

METHOD

PRE-HEAT GRILL

Roll up 12 bacon rashers, place on a skewer or fasten with wooden cocktail sticks, then grill. Remove from the skewer or remove cocktail sticks; place bacon rolls around the turkey with the sausages.

HERB SAUSAGES

Serves 12

INGREDIENTS

1½ lb (700 g) lean pork
8 oz (225 g) pork fat
8 oz (225 g) pie veal
4 oz (100 g) fresh white breadcrumbs
½ oz (10 g) grated nutmeg
garlic clove—juice
1 teaspoon salt
1 teaspoon ground black pepper
½ teaspoon grated lemon rind
½ teaspoon dried marjoram
1 teaspoon dried thyme
1 tablespoon dried sage
clarified butter—for frying

METHOD

Finely mince the pork, pork fat and veal. Put the meat, breadcrumbs, nutmeg, garlic juice, salt, black pepper, lemon rind, marjoram and thyme into a bowl and pound to a paste. Mix in the sage.

Using clean hands form mixture into 24 sausage shapes. Fry in clarified butter until brown. Drain on absorbent white kitchen paper towels.

Keep warm until required. These can be made the day before they are required. Place on non-stick baking parchment and lay apart from each other. Lay a second sheet of baking parchment on top and cover with foil to gently seal. Refrigerate.

To serve place a slice of turkey with forcemeat onto each plate; pour over a little Périgueux sauce. Add a grilled bacon roll and one or two herb sausages.

MARROW PATTIES

HOT OVEN
Gas Mark 7   425°F 220°C

Approximately 20 minutes

1 dampened baking tray
Makes 12

INGREDIENTS
for Pastry:

3 oz (75 g) plain flour
3 oz (75 g) strong plain flour
¼ teaspoon salt
4 oz (100 g) butter—firm but not hard
1 teaspoon lemon juice
iced water
1 small egg—beaten

for Marrow Bone Sauce:

6" (15 cm) length shin of veal
knob butter
1 shallot—finely chopped
1 teaspoon flour
4 tablespoons stock
squeeze lemon juice
6 button mushrooms—finely chopped
pinch grated nutmeg
pinch sugar
1 tablespoon fresh parsley—finely chopped
seasoning

METHOD

Sift the flours and salt into a large bowl. Place the butter in the flour mixture then cut the butter using 2 knives into even pieces about the size of walnuts. Using a round bladed knife quickly stir in the lemon juice and enough iced water to make a soft (but not wet) dough. Turn the mixture out onto a floured working surface and lightly shape into a rectangle then roll out to ¾" (2 cm)

thick. Fold the bottom half of the dough up then fold the upper part down. Turn dough so that the fold is on the left hand side, seal edges lightly. Roll out dough once more this time to ½" (1.3 cm) thickness. Repeat the rolling folding and turning four times. Rest the dough in the refrigerator after the second and fourth rollings wrapped in cling film or cooking foil for 15 minutes each time.

Cover one end of the veal bone with flour and water paste. Place the bone upright (paste side down) in a pan containing hot water reaching half way up the bone, cover with a lid and boil for 25 minutes; when cooked remove the marrow.

Heat the butter in a saucepan add the shallot and sauté until golden. Stir in the flour and cook for 2 minutes; gradually add the stock and lemon juice stir until it begins to thicken and is smooth. Mix in the mushrooms, nutmeg, sugar, parsley, seasoning and the marrow. Remove from the heat and leave to cool.

PRE-HEAT OVEN

Roll out the dough on a floured working surface to a rectangle approximately 6" × 18" (15 × 46 cm). Using a sharp knife, cut rectangle into twelve 3" (7.6 cm) squares. Brush edges of squares with beaten egg. Place a portion of the marrow bone sauce on one half of each square; fold over the other half and press dampened edges together. Place on prepared baking tray and brush over the tops of the patties with beaten egg. Place in the oven and bake until well risen and golden brown. Keep warm until required.

Note: If beef stock is not available for the marrow bone sauce substitute undiluted concentrated tinned consommé.
    The marrow patties can be prepared the day before serving, but do not brush over the tops with beaten egg at this stage. Cover the base of a suitable tray with non-stick baking parchment and place the patties well apart on top. Cover with another sheet of the parchment and then seal in foil. Place in a refrigerator.

ROAST QUAIL ON TOAST

Quail should be hung until the feathers pull out easily above the tail.

It is sometimes possible to buy an oven ready frozen quail. Please read instructions on the wrapper very carefully before defrosting.

HOT OVEN
Gas Mark 7   425°F   220°C

Approximately 30 minutes

INGREDIENTS
12 quail
ground black pepper
6 oz (150 g) soft butter
squeeze lemon juice
12 strips pork fat
vine leaves
2 fl oz (50 ml) dry white wine
12 thick slices of toast cut into small rounds

METHOD
PRE-HEAT OVEN

Blend together the black pepper, butter and lemon juice. Wipe each bird inside and out with a clean damp cloth. Place a little of the butter mixture in the cavity of each bird. Place pork fat on the breasts of the birds then enclose birds in the vine leaves. Place in a roasting tin (do not let the birds touch one another) and pour in the wine. Roast until juices run clean when thighs are pierced with a skewer. Remove vine leaves and pork fat.

Serve each quail on a round of toast and pour some of the juices over each.

FRIARS OMELETTE

Adapted from *Domestic Cookery By A Lady* by Mrs Rundell (1841)

FAIRLY HOT OVEN
Gas Mark 6   400°F 200°C

Approximately 30 minutes

10″ × 2″ (25 × 5 cm) round non-stick cake tin
Serves 12

Prepare the cake tin by spreading the base and sides with 2 oz (50 g) of butter. Melt 4 oz (100 g) of the butter and mix in the breadcrumbs. Now thickly cover the buttered tin with the breadcrumbs keeping some in reserve to put on top of the omelette. Press the breadcrumbs firmly, but gently.

INGREDIENTS

9 oz (250 g) butter
1 lb (450 g) fresh white breadcrumbs
1 lb (450 g) cox's apples
1 lb (450 g) cooking apples
½ lemon—juice and grated rind
2 tablespoons caster sugar
2 large eggs—beaten
icing sugar—sifted
frosted or imitation holly leaves

METHOD

PRE-HEAT OVEN

Core, peel and slice the apples. Once done place them in a large saucepan with the lemon juice and rind, the remaining butter and caster sugar. Simmer gently until the apples soften. Remove from the heat and beat in the eggs. Pour apple mixture into the prepared tin, smooth out evenly with a spatula then cover with the reserved breadcrumbs. Place in the oven. Cook until golden and firm to the touch. Remove from the oven and leave for 7 minutes in the tin.

Put a serving platter upside down over the tin and then turn them quickly both over. Remove the tin leaving the omelette on the platter. Coat very thickly with icing sugar. Arrange holly leaves around the base of the omelette to decorate.

Serve hot or cold cut into wedges.

Note: The breadcrumbed cake tin can be prepared the day before serving. Just cover the top of the tin with cooking foil and place in the refrigerator. The remaining breadcrumbs can be placed loosely in a container.

CLARET JELLY

Serves 12

INGREDIENTS
¼ pint (150 ml) boiling water
4 oz (100 g) fast dissolving sugar cubes
8 tablespoons red currant jelly
1 pint (570 ml) claret
¼ pint (150 ml) brandy
1 oz (25 g) powdered gelatine

METHOD
Pour boiling water into a bowl and dissolve sugar cubes and red currant jelly in it.

Warm the claret and brandy in a saucepan and add to the liquid in the bowl. Stand the bowl over a pan of simmering water (do not let the bowl touch the water). Sprinkle on the powdered gelatine and stir with a metal spoon until dissolved. The spoon will be free of granules when this operation is completed.

To serve claret jelly pour into 12 small glasses; leave to set. This can be made the day before serving.

ACCOMPANIMENTS, PRESERVES, GLAZES AND STOCK

BEETROOT PICKLE

Adapted from Mrs Beeton's *Book Of Household Management* (1911)

INGREDIENTS

6 medium beetroots
2 pints (1 litre) malt vinegar
½ oz (10 g) whole black pepper
½ oz (10 g) allspice
1 small horseradish—grated

METHOD

Wash the beetroots carefully. The skin must not be torn or they will bleed. Cut off the leaf stalks 1–2″ above the root but do not trim the root end until they are cooked. Boil in lightly salted water for about 1½ hours or until they are tender. Drain and when cool enough to handle slide off the skins, cut the beetroots into ½″ (2.5 cm) slices and place them in jars. Meanwhile, boil the vinegar, pepper, spice and horseradish together, let the mixture become quite cold, then pour it over the beetroot. Cover with vinegar proof lids. Store in a cool dry place.

BENTON SAUCE

Adapted from Mrs Beeton's *Book Of Household Management* (1861)

INGREDIENTS

1 tablespoon horseradish—finely grated
1 teaspoon made English mustard
1 teaspoon caster sugar
4 tablespoons vinegar

METHOD

Mix all the ingredients thoroughly together. With cold meat this sauce is a very good substitute for pickles.

Serve with hot or cold Roast Beef.

GREAT GRANDMOTHER'S GREEN TOMATO CHUTNEY

Yields 4½ lb (2 kg)

INGREDIENTS

3 lb (1.35 kg) green tomatoes
1 lb (450 g) onions
salt
2 lb (1 kg) cooking apples
8 oz (225 g) sultanas
½ teaspoon cayenne pepper
½ teaspoon ground ginger
1 oz (25 g) mustard seed
1 pint (570 ml) vinegar

METHOD

Slice the tomatoes and onions and place in a container. Sprinkle salt over them. Leave to stand for 12 hours after which they must drain for 12 hours. Chop the cooking apples and sultanas and place in a large saucepan with the drained tomatoes and all the remaining ingredients. Boil for about 2 hours or until it has the appearance of jam. Pour into warm sterilized jars and use vinegar proof covers.

HORSERADISH SAUCE

INGREDIENTS

2 tablespoons horseradish—fresh or preserved
½ pint (275 ml) double cream
½ teaspoon sugar
1 tablespoon vinegar—only if using fresh horseradish

METHOD

Grate the horseradish as finely as possible. Mix all ingredients together.

PRESERVED HORSERADISH

INGREDIENTS
stick of horseradish
vinegar

METHOD
Peel and grate the horseradish as finely as possible. Pack a jar to the top with horseradish and vinegar. Press down well and cover with a vinegar proof lid.

APPLE JELLY

INGREDIENTS
6 lb (2.7 kg) cooking apples
3 pints (1.7 L) water
1 lb (450 g) preserving sugar
2 lemons — pared rinds and juice

METHOD
Chop the apples into small pieces and place in a large saucepan over a very low heat. Simmer until a pulp. Put the apple pulp and juice in a jelly bag and leave to drip into a bowl overnight. Measure the drained apple juice into a preserving pan allowing 1 lb of sugar to each pint of juice. Tie together the pared lemon rinds and add to the pan with the juice. Bring slowly to the boil, stirring until the sugar has dissolved. Boil rapidly. After several minutes check to see if the jelly is ready by removing the pan from the heat and placing a small quantity on a cold saucer and allowing to cool. If the jelly crinkles lightly when pushed with the finger tip the jelly is ready.

Pour into warm sterilized jars and cover with waxed discs, waxed side down. Seal the jars with cellophane discs and rubber bands or screw-on lids. Label and store in a cool, dry and if possible dark place.

GREAT GRANDMOTHER'S PICKALILLA

INGREDIENTS

1 cauliflower

1 marrow

1 cucumber

1½ lb (700 g) onions

salt

3 pints (1.7 litre) vinegar

12 chillies

12 cloves

3 tablespoons plain flour

9 oz (250 g) demerara sugar

2 tablespoons mustard powder

½ oz (15 g) turmeric

1 oz (25 g) ground ginger

METHOD

Cut the vegetables into small pieces and place in a large container. Sprinkle salt over them. Leave to stand for 12 hours; after which they must drain for 12 hours. Boil together the vinegar, chillies and cloves for 3 minutes. Cool then strain through a sieve. Pour the spiced vinegar into a large saucepan and bring back to the boil. Mix together the flour, sugar, mustard powder, turmeric and ginger into a smooth paste with a little cooled vinegar. Gradually pour the boiling vinegar onto the paste mixture and blend together until smooth. Return vinegar mixture to the saucepan, add the vegetables and boil for 10 minutes.

Pour into warm sterilized jars and use vinegar proof covers.

PICKLED SPANISH ONIONS
Adapted from Mrs Beeton's *Book of Household Management* (1861)

INGREDIENTS

spanish onions
malt vinegar
salt and cayenne pepper — to taste

METHOD

Mix salt and cayenne pepper to taste. Cut the onions into thin slices. Put a layer of them in the bottom of a jar, sprinkle with salt mixture and add another layer of onions and season as before. Proceed in this manner till the jar is full. Then pour in sufficient vinegar to cover the whole. Seal with vinegar proof lids. This pickle will be ready for use in a month.

PICKLED EGGS
Adapted from *Cassell's New Universal Cookery Book* by Lizzie Heritage (1896)

INGREDIENTS

30 eggs
3 pints (1.7 L) vinegar
1 oz (25 g) black peppercorns
1½ oz (35 g) allspice berries
½ oz (10 g) root ginger
1 teaspoon salt

METHOD

Boil a quarter of the vinegar with the spices and salt until reduced by half. Add the remaining vinegar and bring to the boil. Pour over the eggs. The vinegar should come an inch above the eggs.

Seal with vinegar proof covers and leave for one month before using.

Note: These are not only useful as a pickle but also for garnishing many dishes.

TOMATO SAUCE FOR KEEPING

Adapted from Mrs Beeton's *Book of Household Management* (1861)

Makes 2½ lb (1.13 kg)

INGREDIENTS

2½ lb (1.13 kg) ripe tomatoes
1 tablespoon ground ginger
2 teaspoons salt
1 head garlic — juice
2 tablespoons malt vinegar
1 tablespoon chili vinegar — a small quantity of cayenne may be substituted for this

METHOD

Put the tomatoes into a saucepan over a very gentle heat until they are quite tender. When cold remove the skins and stalks, mix the pulp with the liquor in the saucepan but do not strain. Add all the other ingredients. Mix well together and put into sterilized bottles. Cover with vinegar proof lids.

ENGLISH MUSTARD

INGREDIENTS

mustard powder
cold water

METHOD

The secret of good mustard is to see that it is neither lumpy nor sloppy. Stir from the centre with the back of a spoon, adding water by degrees. The mustard should just drop off the spoon. For a very mild mustard, cream or milk is used in the mixing in place of a quarter of the water.

Note: Mustard soon discolours and becomes very unsightly as well as disagreeable to the taste. It should be prepared in the required quantity and always put into a clean dry pot.

CANDIED LEMON AND ORANGE PEEL

INGREDIENTS

1 lb (450 g) peel
4 oz (100 g) granulated sugar
4 oz (100 g) powdered glucose
4 oz (100 g) granulated sugar

METHOD

Wash the fruit thoroughly. Cut each fruit into quarters lengthways, remove the peel and any excess white pith. Put the prepared peel into a saucepan and cover with water. Simmer over a gentle heat uncovered until the peel is soft. This process will take about 1½ hours. Top up with more water if necessary. Drain the peel and reserve the liquid. Place the peel in a heatproof bowl.

Put half a pint of reserved liquid, sugar and glucose into a saucepan over a gentle heat. Stir until the sugar has dissolved. Bring to the boil then pour the hot syrup over the peel making sure the peel is completely immersed. Cover and leave for 48 hours.

Place a sieve over a saucepan and carefully drain the syrup from the peel into the saucepan. Stand the sieve containing the peel on a plate. Add 4 oz of sugar to the syrup, stir over a gentle heat until the sugar has dissolved. Bring to the boil and boil for 1 minute. Add the peel, reduce the heat and simmer uncovered until the peel is nearly transparent. Remove the peel carefully with a slotted spoon and lay it on a wire rack placed over a baking tray to catch the drips. Cover the peel with a sheet of non-stick baking parchment.

To dry the candied peel. Place tray containing the rack and peel in a warm place such as an airing cupboard. Turn the peel occasionally during the drying process. The peel is dry when the surface is no longer sticky.

Store in a cool dark place. Use screw top jars and place peel between layers of waxed paper. This peel is best used within 6 months.

GRATED LEMON PEEL TO STORE
Adapted from *Cassell's New Universal Cookery Book* by Lizzie Heritage (1896)

When lemon juice is wanted and there is no immediate use for the peel, it can be grated and mixed with its bulk of sugar or salt, just according to the nature of the dishes for which it will be used. Put into small glass bottles, cover and keep in a dry place.

Another way is to cover with wine and use for flavouring purposes generally.

Note: The peel must be dried thoroughly by gentle heat, an airing cupboard is ideal.

PEARS PRESERVED WHOLE
Adapted from *Cassell's New Universal Cookery Book* by Lizzie Heritage (1896)

INGREDIENTS
1" (2.5 cm) whole ginger
6 cloves
6 allspice berries
1" (2.5 cm) cinnamon
2 lb (900 g) sugar cubes
1 lemon — juice and rind
3 lb (1.35 kg) small ripe pears — thinly pared
1 tablespoon brandy or port

METHOD
Boil the spices in a little water until the water is flavoured. Strain spiced water into a large saucepan and add the sugar, lemon juice and rind and bring to the boil. Skim off any scum. Add the pears and boil them in the syrup until tender. Put the pears into warm sterilized jars. Add the brandy or port to the syrup, pour syrup mixture over the pears. Cover with suitable lids.

PINEAPPLE PRESERVE

INGREDIENTS

1 lb (450 g) fresh pineapple
1 lb (450 g) preserving sugar

METHOD

Peel, core and cut the pineapple into thick slices and put in a large saucepan with ¼ pint (150 ml) water and simmer until the slices are tender. Remove the pineapple slices. Add the sugar to the water in the saucepan and stir over a gentle heat until the sugar has dissolved. Return the pineapple slices to the syrup and cook over a medium heat until the slices are nearly transparent and the syrup is thick. Leave to cool for 5 minutes then remove the pineapple slices and put them into warm sterilized jars and cover with the syrup. Cover and label.

Keep in a cool dark place.

CHICKEN STOCK

Makes approximately 3 pints (1.7 L)

INGREDIENTS

3½ pints (2 L) water
2 chicken carcasses, including giblets
1 stick celery
1 large carrot
1 large onion
1 sprig fresh parsley
1 teaspoon dried mixed herbs
6 peppercorns
salt

METHOD

Break the chicken carcasses into small pieces. Slice the carrots, celery and onion. Place all the ingredients in a large saucepan. Bring to the boil, reduce heat and simmer for 1 hour. Strain through a sieve into a large bowl. Cover and leave in a refrigerator until cold. Remove fat which will have solidified on the top of the stock.

After the fat has been removed the stock is ready for use.

The stock can now be frozen if you wish. To freeze pour into rigid containers leaving space for expansion. Cover, label and freeze. If the stock has been frozen place it in a saucepan, stirring occasionally and bring slowly to the boil, use as required for recipe.

BEEF STOCK AND GLAZE

This stock is for use with Périgueux Sauce and other brown sauces
Makes approximately 5¼ pints (3.4 L) stock

INGREDIENTS

2 oz (50 g) clarified butter
3½ lb (1.5 kg) beef marrowbones and veal bones
½ lb (225 g) leg of beef — minced
1 oz (25 g) bacon rind
3 oz (75 g) carrot
3 oz (75 g) onion
3 oz (75 g) leek
1 stalk celery
1 flat mushroom
6 black peppercorns
salt
bouquet garni

METHOD

Chop the bones and bacon rind and slice all the vegetables.

Heat the clarified butter in a large saucepan; add the pieces of bone, minced beef and bacon rind then brown them. Towards the end of the browning put in the sliced vegetables; finish browning all ingredients together. This initial browning helps to give a good colour and flavour. Now pour over sufficient cold water to cover the ingredients completely. Add the mushrooms, peppercorns, salt and bouquet garni. Bring slowly to the boil, skimming off any scum with a metal spoon. Cover with a lid, reduce the heat and simmer for 3 hours.

Remove from the heat, take out the bones then strain off the stock into a large bowl using a sieve. Cover and leave in a refrigerator until cold. Remove the fat which will have solidified on the top of the stock. After the fat has been removed the stock is ready for use.

The stock can now be frozen if you wish. To freeze pour into rigid containers leaving space for expansion. Cover, label and freeze.

If the stock has been frozen place it in a saucepan, stirring occasionally and bring slowly to the boil, use as required for recipe.

GLAZE

After the fat has been removed, place 2 pints (1.15 L) of stock in a saucepan over a medium heat, skimming from time to time with a metal spoon. When it becomes syrupy stir until thick. Remove from the heat and pour into a small pot or jar and cover. This glaze should be stored in a refrigerator but it is not recommended that it be kept for too long. Use to enrich gravies, soups and sauces.

ASPIC JELLY

Aspic jelly is a clear jelly the basis of which is a good, strong poultry, meat or fish stock

Makes approximately 2 pints (1.15 L)

INGREDIENTS
2 pints (1.15 l) cold meat, game, fish or poultry stock
4 fl oz (100 ml) egg white
1 fl oz (25 ml) dry white wine
2 fl oz (50 ml) sherry
1 tablespoon wine vinegar
1¾ oz (40 g) powdered gelatine

METHOD
Place cold stock mixture in a large saucepan. Whip the egg white until frothy and add to the stock. Place saucepan over maximum heat and whisk continually bringing to boiling point. Reduce heat: the egg white will separate and float on the top of the stock. Leave to simmer for about 20 minutes. Place a large sieve, covered with a clean piece of muslin, over a fresh saucepan. Gently pour the stock through the muslin-lined sieve. Sprinkle the powdered gelatine onto the cleared stock and stir with a metal spoon until dissolved. If the stock has become too cool to dissolve the gelatine, reheat stock gently and stir until the spoon is free of granules when you lift it out. Cool aspic and use for coating when it is on the point of setting.

AFTERNOON TEA

*During the festive season there are sure to be passing visitors
popping in to pass on the Season's Greetings
and these guests should be given a real Victorian welcome*

SUGARED ALMOND PETTICOAT TAILS

SLOW OVEN
Gas Mark 2   300°F 150°C

Approximately 45–50 minutes

1 lightly buttered baking tray

INGREDIENTS
8oz (225 g) plain flour
2 oz (50 g) caster sugar
pinch salt
5 oz (125 g) butter
2 oz (50 g) almond nibs

PRE-HEAT OVEN

METHOD

Sift together the flour, sugar and salt and place in a bowl. Rub in the butter until the mixture resembles breadcrumbs, mix in the almond nibs. Knead dough lightly until a ball and place on prepared baking tray; gently roll and press into an 8″ (20 cm) circle. Mark out 8 portions with the blade of a knife without cutting right through to the base. Place in the oven. Bake until a pale straw colour. Leave to cool a little on the baking tray then cut through the markings. Cool the almond petticoat tails on a wire rack. Dust with caster sugar.

Note: Store in an airtight container.

RATAFIAS

SLOW OVEN
Gas Mark 2   270°F 135°C

Approximately 15 minutes

2 large baking trays lined with pure non-stick baking parchment
Makes about 175

INGREDIENTS

1 oz (25 g) rice flour
2 oz (50 g) ground almonds
4 oz (100 g) caster sugar
1 large egg white
natural almond essence — to taste

PRE-HEAT OVEN

METHOD

Mix together the rice flour, ground almonds and caster sugar and place in a bowl. Lightly whisk the egg white and add to the bowl with the almond essence. Using a round bladed knife mix ingredients to form a soft paste. Roll ¼ teaspoonfuls of the mixture into tiny balls and place on baking trays. Sprinkle cakes with caster sugar. Bake until Ratafias are a very pale golden colour. Cool on wire racks.

Note: Ratafias will keep for many weeks in an airtight container.

GREAT GRANDMOTHER'S FROSTED GENOESE CAKE

MODERATE OVEN
Gas Mark 4   350°F 180°C

Approximately 20 minutes

3 non-stick sponge tins 7¼″ (18.5 cm) buttered and bases lined with greaseproof paper

INGREDIENTS
4 large eggs
8 oz (225 g) caster sugar
2 tablespoons brandy
8 oz (225 g) plain flour
large pinch salt
8 oz (225 g) butter — just melted not oily
8 oz (225 g) marmalade

for the Frosting:

4 oz (100 g) caster sugar
12 oz (350 g) icing sugar — sifted
2 medium egg whites
few drops orange food colouring

PRE-HEAT OVEN

METHOD
Sift together the flour and salt. Whisk the eggs and sugar in a large bowl over hot water until thick (do not allow the bowl to touch the water); still whisking add the brandy. Remove the bowl from the heat and continue whisking until the mixture is cold. Using a balloon whisk fold in two thirds of the flour mixture then fold in the butter and the remaining flour mixture. Spread the mixture out gently, but evenly between the 3 prepared sponge tins. Place in the oven; bake until golden and firm to the touch. Turn cakes out onto damp cloth and leave until cold.

Remove greaseproof paper from the base of each cake. Put one Genoese cake onto an ovenproof cake plate. Divide the marmalade into two portions; sandwich the three cakes together with the marmalade. Sift the icing sugar for the frosting into a bowl with all the other ingredients and whisk until thick. Cover the top and sides of the cake with frosting. Place cake back in the oven for 1 minute (no longer) at Gas mark 2 300°F150° C. Leave until cold.

HUNTING NUTS

Adapted from *Warne's Model Cookery and Housekeeping Book compiled and edited by Mary Jewry* (c.1880)

SLOW OVEN
Gas Mark 2   300°F 150°C

Approximately 12 minutes

2 large baking trays lined with non-stick pure baking parchment
Makes about 300

INGREDIENTS

3 oz (75 g) butter
8 oz (225 g) self-raising flour — sifted
4 oz (100 g) treacle
4 oz (100 g) demerara sugar
3 tablespoons ground ginger

PRE-HEAT OVEN

METHOD

Melt the butter and mix in a bowl with the sifted flour. Add all the remaining ingredients and knead together using one hand for about a minute. Next roll small amounts of the mixture between clean hands into tiny balls about ½" (1.3 cm) in diameter and place them on trays allowing room for the mixture to spread. They should be but the size of a shilling (5 pence piece) when cooked. Cool on wire trays.

Note: These are excellent and keep very well in an airtight container.

VICTORIA BISCUITS WITH GLACE ICING
Adapted from the Cook's Guide by Charles Elmé Francatelli (1888)

SLOW OVEN
Gas Mark 2   300°F 150°C

Approximately 15 minutes

2 large lightly buttered baking trays
Makes about 50

INGREDIENTS

3 oz (75 g) soft butter
8 oz (225 g) caster sugar
5 tablespoons Kirsch
6 oz (150 g) plain flour
3 oz (75 g) ground almonds
pinch salt
1 lemon — grated rind
marmalade

PRE-HEAT OVEN

METHOD

Cream butter and sugar together then beat in the Kirsch. Sift the flour and add with the ground almonds, salt and lemon rind. Roll out to 1/6″ (4 mm) thick. Cut out rounds with a 2″ (5 cm) pastry cutter. Place rounds on the prepared trays and prick each round with a fork. Bake until a very pale colour. Cool on wire racks. When they have cooled spread about ½ teaspoon of marmalade on the top of each biscuit then spoon glacé icing over the top of the biscuits.

GLACE ICING

To make Glacé Icing place 8 oz (225 g) sifted icing sugar in a bowl. Add 3 tablespoons of hot, almost boiling water, a little at a time until the icing coats the back of a wooden spoon.

GREAT GRANDMOTHER'S MACAROON BITES

SLOW OVEN
Gas Mark 2   300°F 150°C

Approximately 15 minutes

2 large baking trays lined with rice paper
Makes about 48

INGREDIENTS
2 large egg whites
½ teaspoon vanilla essence
4 oz (100 g) caster sugar
1 oz (25 g) icing sugar
¼ teaspoon cream of tartar
4 oz (100 g) desiccated coconut
2 oz (50 g) walnuts — chopped

PRE-HEAT OVEN

METHOD

Sift together the icing sugar and cream of tartar and mix with the caster sugar.
Whisk the egg whites until stiff. Add the vanilla essence to the whisked egg
whites then whisking continually gradually add the sugar mixture. When the
mixture is stiff fold in the coconut and chopped walnuts. Place spoonfuls of the
mixture (the size of a walnut) onto the prepared trays. Place in the oven and
bake until lightly coloured. Cool on wire racks and remove surplus rice paper
when the bites are cold.

ECCLES CAKES

HOT OVEN
Gas Mark 7   425°F 220°C

Approximately 15 minutes

A large dampened baking tray
Makes about 18

INGREDIENTS
for Rough Puff Pastry:

4 oz (100 g) plain flour
4 oz (100 g) strong plain flour
1 teaspoon salt
6 oz (150 g) butter — firm but not hard
1 teaspoon lemon juice
iced water
1 large egg — beaten
caster sugar

for the Filling:

2 oz (50 g) soft butter
5 oz (125 g) currants
lemon — grated rind
orange — grated rind
1 oz (25 g) candied lemon/orange peel — chopped
1 oz (25 g) moist brown sugar
½ teaspoon grated nutmeg
½ teaspoon mixed spice
pinch cinnamon

PRE-HEAT OVEN

METHOD
Sift the flours and salt into a large bowl. Place the butter in the flour mixture then cut the butter using two knives into even pieces about the size of walnuts.

Using a round-bladed knife quickly stir in the lemon juice and enough iced water to make a soft (but not wet) dough. Turn dough out onto a floured working surface and knead it lightly. Shape into a rectangle then roll out to ¾" (2 cm) thick. Fold the bottom half of the dough up and then fold the upper part down. Turn dough so that the fold is on the left hand side, seal edges lightly. Roll out dough once more this time to ½" (1.5 cm) thickness. Repeat the rolling, folding and turning 4 times. Rest the dough in the refrigerator after second and fourth rollings wrapped in cling film or cooking foil for 15 minutes each time.

Mix all the ingredients for the filling together.

Roll dough out to about ¼" (6 cm) thick and cut out rounds using a 3½" (8 cm) pastry cutter. Place rounds onto prepared tray and put an equal portion of the filling in the centre of each dough round. Dampen the edges with beaten egg and gather up into a ball shape; turn over and gently roll out until the fruit begins to show through. Make two or three slits in the top and brush with beaten egg then sprinkle with caster sugar. Place in the oven and bake until well risen and golden brown. Cool on a wire rack.

MAIDS OF HONOUR

Adapted from Mrs Beeton's *Book of Household Management* (1911)

HOT OVEN
Gas Mark 7   425°F 220°C

Approximately 10 minutes

12 hole non-stick patty pan

INGREDIENTS

3 oz (75 g) plain flour
3 oz (75 g) strong plain flour
¼ teaspoon salt
4 oz (100 g) butter — firm but not hard
1 teaspoon lemon juice
iced water

for the Filling:

raspberry jam
3 oz (75 g) ground almonds
2½ oz (65 g) caster sugar
2½ tablespoons double cream
2 large eggs
1 oz (25 g) self raising flour
1 tablespoon orange water

METHOD

PRE-HEAT OVEN

Sift the flours and salt into a large bowl; place the butter in the flour then cut the butter, using 2 knives, into even sized pieces about the size of walnuts. Using a round-bladed knife quickly stir in the lemon juice and enough iced water to make a soft (but not wet) dough. Turn the mixture out onto a floured working surface and lightly shape into a rectangle then roll out to ¾" (2 cm) thick. Fold the bottom half of the dough up and then fold the upper part down. Turn dough so that the fold is on the left hand side, seal edges lightly. Roll out dough once more this time to ½" (1.3 cm) thickness. Repeat the rolling, folding and turning 4 times. Rest the dough in the refrigerator after the second and fourth rollings wrapped in cling film or cooking foil for 15 minutes each time.

Roll out the dough on a floured working surface to a rectangle 6″ × 18″ (15 × 45 cm) and cut out 12 rounds using a 3″ (7.6 cm) pastry cutter. Line patty tins with the dough rounds and place a little raspberry jam in the base of each.

Mix together the almonds, caster sugar, double cream, eggs, self-raising flour and orange water and divide into 12 equal portions placing each on top of the jam. Bake in the oven until well risen and golden.

LADY ABBESSES
Adapted from Domestic Cookery By A Lady *by Mrs Rundell (1841)*

SLOW OVEN
Gas Mark 2   300°F 150°C

Approximately 14 minutes

12 hole non-stick sheet of patty pans thickly buttered

INGREDIENTS
3 oz (75 g) ground almonds
2 oz (50 g) caster sugar
½ oz (10 g) butter
1½ tablespoons rosewater
jam
6 tablespoons whipped double cream

PRE-HEAT OVEN

METHOD
Pound the ground almonds, sugar, butter and rosewater in a mortar until it becomes a thick paste. Divide the paste into 12 equal portions and press into the patty tins to cover using the middle finger. Place in the oven and bake until a pale golden colour and firm to the touch. Leave to cool in the pans then ease out. Top with a little jam and a teaspoon of cream.

MUFFINS

Heavy frying pan or griddle — greased
Makes 12

INGREDIENTS

½ pint (275 ml) milk — heat until tepid
½ oz (10 g) fresh yeast
1 oz (25 g) melted butter
1 large egg
1 lb (450 g) plain flour
1 teaspoon salt

METHOD

Heat the milk until tepid and divide in half. Into one half whisk the yeast until creamy and blend the other half with the melted butter and egg. Then blend the 2 milk mixtures together. Sift the flour with the salt in a large bowl and add the combined milk mixture. Mix to a soft dough. Turn dough out onto a lightly floured working surface and knead until smooth and elastic. Place in a greased bowl, cover and leave in a warm place to double in size. Turn dough out once more onto a lightly floured working surface and knead lightly. Roll dough out and cut out 12 rounds with a 3″ (7.5 cm) pastry cutter. Place on prepared tray and dust the tops with flour. Cover and leave in a warm place to double in size again.

Cook muffins, a few at a time, in a greased heavy frying pan or on a greased griddle over a moderate heat until slightly brown on both sides.

To serve, divide each muffin by pulling it open all around the edges with the fingers. Butter them lightly on both sides, put muffins together again then cut into halves. Pile them on a very hot dish and serve immediately.

GREAT GRANDMOTHER'S SCONES

HOT OVEN
Gas Mark 7   450°F 230°C

Approximately 10 minutes for small scones.
If making 1 large scone reduce the heat after 10 minutes
to Gas Mark 5   375°F 190°C and bake a further 10 minutes

1 non-stick baking tray
Makes 12 small or 1 large scone

INGREDIENTS

8 oz (225 g) plain flour
½ teaspoon bicarbonate of soda
1 teaspoon cream of tartar — ½ if sour milk is used
¼ teaspoon salt
1½ oz (35 g) butter — firm cut into small pieces
1 tablespoon caster sugar
scant ¼ pint (150 ml) milk
jam
whipped double cream

METHOD

PRE-HEAT OVEN

Sift together the flour, bicarbonate, cream of tartar and salt. Place flour mixture in a large bowl then add the butter and rub in until the mixture resembles breadcrumbs; mix in the caster sugar then gradually add the milk and mix to a soft (but not wet) dough using a round-bladed knife. Knead lightly on a floured working surface and roll out to a ½″ (1.5 cm) thickness. Cut out 12 rounds with a 2″ (5 cm) pastry cutter and place rounds (or roll out into 1 large round ½″ (1.5 cm) thick on baking tray; brush with milk and place in the preheated oven; bake until well risen and golden. Cool on a wire rack.

Serve scones with jam and whipped cream.

Note: These are best eaten on the day they are baked. If sour milk is used a better result is achieved.

SALLY LUNNS

HOT OVEN
Gas Mark 8   450°F 230°C

Approximately 15–20 minutes

2 round cake tins 5″ (13 cm) thickly buttered

INGREDIENTS
2 oz (50 g) butter
¼ pint (150 ml) milk
2 fl oz (50 ml) single cream
1 teaspoon caster sugar
½ oz (10 g) fresh yeast
2 medium eggs — beaten
1 lb (450 g) strong plain white flour
1 teaspoon salt

METHOD
Blend together the milk, cream and caster sugar. Melt the butter in a saucepan then add the milk mixture and heat until just lukewarm. Remove saucepan from the heat and stir in the beaten eggs, then add the yeast and whisk until creamy. Sift together the flour and salt in a large bowl. Add the milk mixture and work into a soft dough. Turn dough out onto a floured working surface and knead until smooth. Divide dough in half and knead into 2 ball shapes. Place dough in the 2 prepared tins. Cover with buttered cling film then with a clean cloth. Leave in a warm place until dough rises to the top of the tins.

PRE-HEAT OVEN

Remove cloth and cling film. Place in preheated oven and bake until golden approximately 15–20 minutes. Turn out onto wire racks. Place 2 tablespoons of caster sugar and 2 tablespoons of water in a saucepan and boil for 2 minutes. Brush over the top of the Sally Lunns when they are still hot.

To serve cut off the top of each Sally Lunn and place about 3 oz (75 g) butter on the cut surface. Replace lids and serve hot.

WHITE GINGERBREAD

MODERATE OVEN
Gas Mark 3   325°F   160°C

Approximately 10 minutes

2 large baking trays lined with non-stick baking parchment
Makes about 60

INGREDIENTS
6 oz (150 g) butter
12 oz (350 g) plain flour
2 tablespoons ground ginger
¼ teaspoon ground mace
¼ teaspoon cream of tartar
pinch salt
6 oz (150 g) caster sugar
½ teaspoon grated lemon rind
1 oz (25 g) candied lemon peel — finely chopped
8 tablespoons milk
¼ teaspoon bicarbonate of soda
1 large egg — beaten

PRE-HEAT OVEN

METHOD
Sift together the flour, ginger, mace, cream of tartar and salt. Rub the butter into the flour mixture until it resembles breadcrumbs then add the sugar, grated lemon rind and the candied peel. Heat the milk until just tepid and dissolve the bicarbonate of soda in it. Add the beaten egg and the milk to the breadcrumb mixture and work into a smooth paste. Roll out to ¼″ (6 mm) thickness then cut into 2″ (5 cm) rounds with a pastry cutter. Place on the trays and bake in preheated oven until just firm to the touch. Cool on wire racks.

Store in an airtight container.

GREAT GRANDMOTHER'S CHOCOLATE CAKE

FAIRLY HOT OVEN
Gas Mark 5   375°F 190°C

Approximately 20 minutes

2 non-stick sandwich cake tins 9½″ (24 cm) buttered and bases lined with greaseproof paper

INGREDIENTS
6 oz (150 g) soft butter
5 oz (125 g) warm caster sugar
1 teaspoon Camp coffee essence
3 large eggs
5 oz (125 g) self-raising flour
2 tablespoons cornflour
2 tablespoons cocoa
1 teaspoon baking powder
¼ teaspoon cinnamon
2 tablespoons boiling water
½ pint (275 ml) double cream — whipped

for the Butter Cream Coating:

5 oz (125 g) soft butter
10 oz (275 g) icing sugar
1 tablespoon cocoa
2 oz (50 g) plain chocolate — melted
2 tablespoons Curaçao

METHOD

PRE-HEAT OVEN

Sift together the flour, cornflour, cocoa, baking powder and cinnamon. Warm the sugar for no more than a few seconds in the oven. Cream the butter and sugar until light and fluffy then whisk in the first egg. As soon as this is incorporated whisk in the second and then the third egg. Still whisking add the Camp essence then fold in the flour mixture using a balloon whisk. Quickly fold in 2 tablespoons of boiling water.

Divide the mixture evenly between the two prepared tins and spread the mixture out gently. Place in the oven. Bake until risen and firm to the touch. Turn cakes out onto wire racks and leave until cold.

To make the butter cream coating. Cream the butter until light and fluffy. Sift together the icing sugar with the cocoa and gradually beat into the melted chocolate and Curaçoa.

Remove greaseproof paper from the base of each cake. Place one cake on a cake stand or plate. Sandwich the two cakes together with the whipped cream. Spread the chocolate orange butter cream over the top and sides of the cake. Leave in a cool place until the butter cream feels firms to the touch then dust with sifted icing sugar.

GREAT GRANDMOTHER'S CHOCOLATE SPONGE CAKE

FAIRLY HOT OVEN
Gas Mark 5   375°F   190°C

Approximately 15 minutes

2 non-stick sandwich cake tins 9½″ (24 cm) buttered and bases lined with greaseproof paper

INGREDIENTS

for the cake:

3 large eggs
5 oz (125 g) caster sugar
1 teaspoon Camp coffee essence
3 oz (75 g) plain flour
1½ oz (40 g) cornflour
2 tablespoons cocoa
¼ teaspoon cinnamon
1 tablespoon baking powder
pinch salt
2 tablespoons hot butter

for the Chocolate Cream:

½ pint (275 ml) double cream
2 tablespoons icing sugar
3 tablespoons cocoa
½ teaspoon Camp coffee essence

PRE-HEAT OVEN

METHOD

Sift together the flour, cornflour, cocoa, cinnamon, baking powder and salt. Whisk the eggs and caster sugar in a bowl over hot water until the mixture is thick (do not allow the bowl to touch the water); still whisking add the Camp essence. Remove the bowl from the heat and continue whisking until mixture is cold. Using a balloon whisk fold in the flour mixture; then quickly fold in the hot butter. Divide the mixture evenly between the prepared tins and shake gently to spread the mixture out. Place in the oven; bake until risen and firm to the touch. Turn cakes out onto wire racks and leave until cold. Remove greaseproof paper.

To make the chocolate cream sift together the cocoa and icing sugar. Then whisk in all other ingredients until thick.

Place one sponge cake on a cake stand or plate. Sandwich the two sponges together with the chocolate cream filling. Dredge the top of the cake thickly with sifted icing sugar.

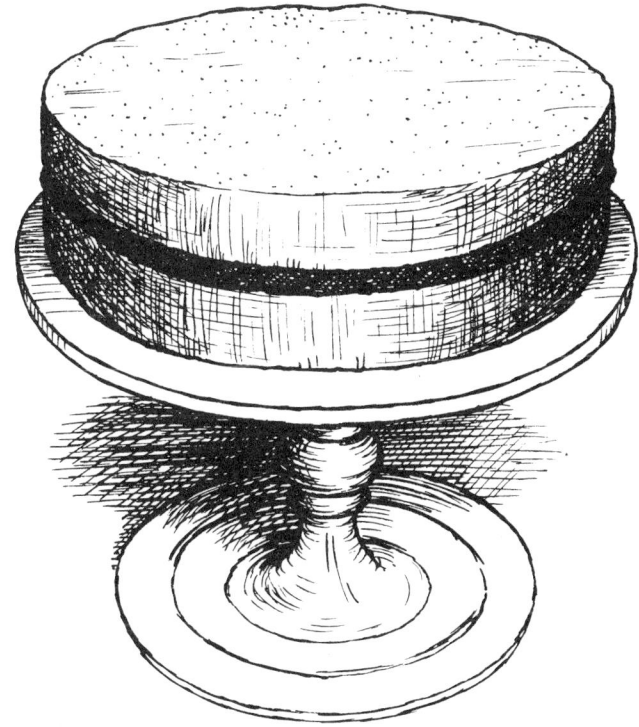

TEA CAKES

FAIRLY HOT OVEN
Gas Mark 6   400°F 200°C

Approximately 20 minutes

Lightly greased baking trays — leave plenty of room between cakes to allow the cakes to spread
Makes 5

INGREDIENTS
1 lb (450 g) strong plain white flour
1 teaspoon salt
2 tablespoons caster sugar
1 oz (25 g) lard
3 oz (75 g) currants
½ pint (275 ml) lukewarm milk
½ oz (10 g) fresh yeast
1 large egg — beaten

METHOD
Sift together the flour and salt in a large bowl. Add the caster sugar then rub in the lard. Mix in the currants. Whisk the milk and yeast until creamy, blend in the beaten egg and stir into the flour mixture to form a soft dough. Turn dough out onto a lightly-floured working surface and knead until smooth and elastic. Place dough in a greased plastic bag and leave to double in size in a warm place. Turn dough out onto a lightly-floured working surface and knead lightly. Divide into 5 equal portions and roll into 6½″ (16.5 cm) round flat cakes. Place cakes on prepared baking trays; glaze with a little milk, cover with lightly greased cling film and leave to double in size.

PRE-HEAT OVEN

Bake in preheated oven for about 20 minutes until golden brown. Turn out onto wire racks.

Note: These cakes should be split buttered and eaten hot as soon as they are baked. If they are allowed to cool and are kept for a period they are very nice toasted.

VICTORIA SANDWICH

FAIRLY HOT OVEN
Gas Mark 5   375°F   190°C

Approximately 20 minutes

2 non-stick sandwich cake tins 9½″ (24 cm) buttered and bases lined with greaseproof paper

INGREDIENTS
6 oz (175 g) soft butter
6 oz (175 g) caster sugar
3 large eggs
5 oz (150 g) self-raising flour
1 oz (25 g) cornflour
½ teaspoon vanilla essence
1 tablespoon boiling water

METHOD
PRE-HEAT OVEN

Sift together the flour and cornflour. Warm the sugar for no more than a few seconds in the oven. Cream the butter and sugar until light and fluffy then whisk in the first egg. As soon as this is incorporated whisk in the second and then the third egg. Still whisking add the vanilla essence then fold in the flour mixture using a balloon whisk. Quickly fold in the boiling water. Divide the mixture evenly between the 2 prepared tins then spread out gently. Place in the oven. Bake until firm to the touch. Turn cakes out onto wire racks to cool. Remove greaseproof paper.

Place one cake on a cake stand or plate. Sandwich the two cakes together with jam of your choice. Dust the top with caster sugar.

SEED CAKE

Adapted from Cassell's *New Universal Cookery Book* by Lizzie Heritage (1896)

MODERATE OVEN
Gas Mark 4   350°F   180°C

Approximately 1 hour 5 minutes

7″ × 3″ (18 × 7.5 cm) round non-stick cake tin base buttered and lined with greaseproof paper

INGREDIENTS

6½ oz (185 g) soft butter
6 oz (175 g) warm caster sugar
3 large eggs
1 tablespoon caraway seeds
¼ teaspoon ground ginger
7 oz (200 g) plain flour
1 oz (25 g) cornflour
1 teaspoon baking powder
2 tablespoons lemon juice
1 teaspoon grated lemon rind
1 tablespoon hot water

METHOD

PRE-HEAT OVEN

Sift together the ginger, flour, cornflour and baking powder. Warm the caster sugar for no more than a few seconds in the oven. Cream the butter and sugar until light and fluffy then whisk in the first egg. As soon as this is incorporated whisk in the second and then the third egg. Using a balloon whisk fold in the caraway seeds then the flour mixture followed by the lemon juice and rind. Quickly fold in the hot water. Pour the mixture into the prepared cake tin, smooth the top and then make a slight hollow in the centre (this helps to give a flat surface to the finished cake). Place in the oven and bake until firm to the touch.

Turn cake out onto a wire rack to cool. Remove greaseproof paper.

SHREWSBURY CAKES

MODERATE OVEN
Gas Mark 4   350°F   180°C

Approximately 11 minutes

2 large baking trays lightly buttered
Makes about 24

INGREDIENTS

6 oz (150 g) soft butter
4 oz (100 g) caster sugar
½ grated lemon rind
1 large egg — beaten
3 tablespoons double cream
3 tablespoons rose water
11½ oz (340 g) self-raising flour
½ teaspoon ground mace
pinch salt

METHOD

Sift together the flour, mace and salt. Cream the butter and sugar together until light and fluffy then gradually beat in the grated lemon rind, egg, cream and rosewater. Using a round-bladed knife stir in the flour mixture making a soft dough. Lightly knead the dough. Place dough in the refrigerator wrapped in cling film and leave to rest for 1 hour 15 minutes.

PRE-HEAT OVEN

Place dough on a well floured working surface and flour rolling pin. Roll out to ¼" (6 mm) thick and cut out 2½" (6.5 cm) rounds with a pastry cutter. These will spread during baking. Place in preheated oven and bake until pale cream in colour.

Cool on wire racks.

Note: These are better when eaten freshly made but do keep very well in an airtight container.

SPONGE CAKE

MODERATE OVEN
Gas Mark 4   350°F 180°C

Approximately 50 minutes

7" × 3" (17.8 × 7.6 cm) cake tin. Lightly butter the whole of the interior of the tin then dust with
a mixture of sifted flour and caster sugar

INGREDIENTS

3 large eggs
4 oz (100 g) caster sugar
3 oz (75 g) plain flour
1 oz (25 g) cornflour
pinch salt
¼ teaspoon baking powder
1 tablespoon hot butter

METHOD
PRE-HEAT OVEN

Sift together the flour, cornflour, salt and baking powder. Whisk the eggs and
sugar in a large bowl over a pan of hot water until thick (do not allow the bowl
to touch the water). Remove the bowl from the heat and continue whisking
until the mixture is cold. Using a balloon whisk fold in the flour mixture then
quickly fold in the hot butter. Pour the mixture into greased tin. Place in the
oven and bake until firm to the touch. Turn sponge cake out onto a wire rack
and leave until cold.

Slice when cool and spread the bottom half with jam or filling to choice.
Sandwich the 2 halves together and cover the top of the cake with a sprinkling of
caster sugar.

MADEIRA CAKE

MODERATE OVEN
Gas Mark 4   350°F 180°C

Approximately 1 hour 5 minutes

7″ × 3″ (18 × 7.5 cm) round non-stick cake tin – base buttered and lined with greaseproof paper

INGREDIENTS

6 oz (150 g) soft butter
6 oz (150 g) warm caster sugar
3 large eggs
7 oz (175 g) plain flour
1 oz (25 g) cornflour
1 teaspoon baking powder
2 tablespoons lemon juice
1 teaspoon grated lemon rind
small piece candied lemon peel

METHOD

PRE-HEAT OVEN

Sift together the flour, cornflour and baking powder. Warm the sugar for no longer than a few seconds in the oven. Cream the butter and sugar until light and fluffy then whisk in the first egg; as soon as this is incorporated whisk in the second and then the third egg. Using a balloon whisk, fold in the flour mixture then the lemon juice and rind. Quickly fold in the hot water. Pour the mixture into prepared cake tin, smooth the top and then make a slight hollow in the centre (this helps to give a flat surface to the finished cake). Place in the oven; after 25 minutes open the oven door and quickly place the piece of candied lemon peel on the top of the cake. Bake until firm to the touch.

Turn cake out onto a wire rack to cool. Remove greaseproof paper.

GREAT GRANDMOTHER'S FROSTED ALMOND AND WALNUT CAKE

FAIRLY HOT OVEN
Gas Mark 5   375°F   190°C

Approximately 20 minutes

2 sandwich cake tins 9½″ (24 cm) lightly buttered with the bases lined with greaseproof paper

INGREDIENTS
for the Cake:

6 oz (150 g) soft butter
6 oz (150 g) warm caster sugar
½ teaspoon almond essence
3 large eggs
2 oz (50 g) chopped walnuts
5 oz (125 g) self-raising flour
1 oz (25 g) cornflour
pinch salt
1 oz (25 g) ground almonds

for the Butter Cream:

4 oz (100 g) soft butter
4½ oz (105 g) icing sugar
¼ teaspoon almond essence

for the Frosting:

4 oz (100 g) caster sugar
12 oz (350 g) icing sugar
2 medium egg whites

METHOD

PRE-HEAT OVEN

Sift together the flour, cornflour and salt and mix with the ground almonds. Warm the caster sugar for no more than a few seconds in the oven. Cream the butter and sugar until light and fluffy then whisk in the first egg. As soon as this is incorporated whisk in the second and then the third. Still whisking add the almond essence then fold in the chopped walnuts and the flour mixture using a balloon whisk. Quickly fold in 1 tablespoon of boiling water. Divide the mixture evenly between the 2 prepared tins and spread the mixture out gently. Place in the oven. Bake until golden and firm to the touch. Turn cakes out onto wire racks and leave until cold.

To make the butter cream sift the icing sugar into a bowl with the butter and almond essence, and mix together until smooth.

To make the frosting sift the icing sugar into a bowl with the caster sugar and the egg whites and whisk until thick.

Remove the greaseproof paper from the base of each cake. Sandwich the two cakes together with the almond butter cream. Place the cake on an ovenproof serving plate. Cover the top and sides of the cake with the frosting and decorate with walnut halves. Put the finished cake in the oven for 1 minute, no longer at Gas Mark 2 300° F 150° C.

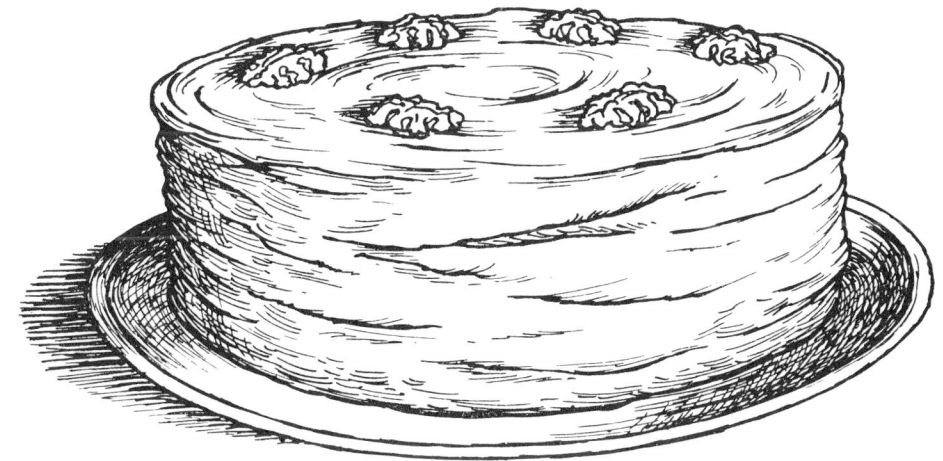

ALMOND MACAROONS

Adapted from Mrs Beeton's *Book of Household Management* (1861)

SLOW OVEN
Gas Mark 2   300°F 150°C

Approximately 15–20 minutes

2 large baking trays lined with rice paper
Makes about 35

INGREDIENTS

8 oz (225 g) caster sugar
8 oz (225 g) ground almonds
3 large egg whites
¼ teaspoon almond essence
split almonds

METHOD

PRE-HEAT OVEN

Whisk the egg whites to a stiff froth. Mix together the caster sugar and ground almonds. Stir caster sugar mixture and the whisked egg whites together, then blend in the almond essence. Put dessertspoonfuls of the mixture on the prepared trays and place a split almond on the top of each portion of the mixture; sprinkle a little caster sugar over the mixture then place in the preheated oven. Bake until risen and a light golden colour.

Cool on wire racks and remove surplus rice paper when the macaroons are cold.

Note: Store in an airtight container.

MADEIRA SANDWICHES

Adapted from *Cassell's New Universal Cookery Book* by Lizzie Heritage (1896)

INGREDIENTS

Madeira cake a day or two old
apple jelly or marmalade
whipped double cream
clear honey
almond nibs

METHOD

Cut the Madeira cake into dainty fingers or other shapes. Allow 3 pieces for each sandwich. On the bottom slice put a layer of apple jelly or marmalade, then lay a second slice on and spread it with cream; put the third slice on very lightly and just smear it with clear honey. Strew with almond nibs.

DRINKS, SWEETS AND CANDY

BARLEY WATER

Adapted from *Domestic Cookery By A Lady* by Mrs Rundell (1841)

INGREDIENTS

1 oz (25 g) pearl barley
½ oz (10 g) caster sugar
1 lemon
2 pints (1 litre) boiling water
1 slice of lemon (optional)

METHOD

Pare rind from lemon. Put pearl barley, sugar, lemon rind and boiling water into a jug. Cover and leave for 8 hours then strain off the liquid, adding a slice of lemon if desired.

BRANDY SHRUB

INGREDIENTS

2 pints (1 litre) brandy
3 lemons
1½ pints (845 ml) white wine
12 oz (350 g) sugar cubes
½ teaspoon grated nutmeg

METHOD

Grate 2 lemons and squeeze juice from all 3 lemons. Mix the brandy, lemon juice and grated rinds together; place in a demijohn (glass fermentation vessel); cork it and let it stand three days, then add the white wine, sugar and nutmeg. Decant the brandy shrub and it is ready for use.

Serve cold.

COLD PUNCH

INGREDIENTS
8 oz (225 g) caster sugar
½ pint (275 ml) water
1 large lemon
2 glasses Curaçoa
1 bottle rum
1 bottle Champagne
few ice cubes

METHOD
Very thinly pare lemon and extract the juice. Put the sugar into a punch bowl with the water and the pared lemon rind. When the sugar has dissolved add the spirits and the lemon juice. Just before serving add the Champagne and a few ice cubes.

HOT PUNCH

INGREDIENTS
2 oz (50 g) sugar cubes
2 lemons
1½ pints (845 ml) boiling water
¾ pint (425 ml) rum
¼ pint (150 ml) brandy
large pinch grated nutmeg

METHOD
Cut off 3 or 4 slices from lemons and rub the sugar cubes over the lemon rinds until they are soaked with the oil. Squeeze the juice from remainder of lemons. Put the sugar cubes in a large punch bowl with the lemon juice. Pour the boiling water over the sugar mixture then add the rum, brandy and nutmeg. Put in the slices of lemon which will float on the top of the punch.

FINE LEMONADE

Adapted from *Domestic Cookery By A Lady* by Mrs Rundell (1841)

INGREDIENTS
4 lemons
8 oz (225 g) sugar cubes
½ pint (275 ml) sherry
2 pints (1.15 L) boiling water
½ pint (275 ml) milk

METHOD
Thinly pare rind of 3 lemons, then extract the juice from all 4. Put the lemon juice, rinds, sugar, sherry and 2 pints of boiling water into a large bowl. Cover and leave for 12 hours. Pour boiling milk into the lemonade then run it through a jelly-bag until it is clear.

MULLED CLARET

INGREDIENTS
½ teaspoon ground cinnamon
½" (1.25 cm) root ginger — bruised
6 cloves
large pinch grated nutmeg
½ pint (275 ml) water
7 oz (200 g) sugar cubes
2 bottles claret
1 orange

METHOD
Remove rind from orange, avoiding pith. Boil the spices in the water until the flavour is extracted; add the sugar, wine and orange rind and bring to the boil.

Serve hot.

NEGUS

Negus derives its name from its originator, Colonel Negus

INGREDIENTS

1½ pints (845 ml) port
2 oz (50 g) sugar cubes
½ teaspoon ground cloves, ground mace
pinch grated nutmeg
1 lemon
3 pints (1.7 L) boiling water

METHOD

Cut lemon into slices. Place port, sugar, mixed spice, nutmeg and lemon slices in a large bowl and pour boiling water over the ingredients.

May be served hot or cold.

BARLEY SUGAR

Adapted from the *Cook's Guide* by Charles Elmé Francatelli (1888)
Makes about 1 lb (450 g)

INGREDIENTS

1 lb (450 g) preserving sugar
¼ pint (150 ml) water
few drops essence of lemon
1 teaspoon citric acid.

METHOD

In a heavy based saucepan gently dissolve the sugar in the water. Boil to the snap (310°F 154°C); add the essence of lemon and citric acid; work the sugar on a lightly-oiled cold surface with 2 knives by merely lifting it together in a heap. When sufficiently cooled pull it into strips. Cut it into 6" (15 cm) lengths; twist these to resemble cord then leave to cool. Store in an airtight glass jar as soon as these are cold.

COCONUT ICE

7" × 7" (19 × 19 cm) non-stick shallow tin, buttered
Makes about 1¼ lb (560 g)

INGREDIENTS

1 lb (450 g) granulated sugar
¼ pint (150 ml) full cream milk
5 oz (125 g) desiccated coconut
few drops pink food colouring

METHOD

Place the sugar and the milk in a heavy based saucepan over a gentle heat and stir until the sugar has dissolved. Bring to the boil and boil steadily until the soft ball stage on a candy thermometer is reached (235°F 113°C). Stir occasionally. Remove the pan from the heat and quickly stir in the coconut. Pour half of the mixture into the prepared tin making sure it is spread out evenly. Stir the food colouring into the remaining mixture in the pan then spread this mixture over the first layer in the tin; smooth over the top with a palette knife. When set the coconut ice can be cut into bars or slices. Store between layers of waxed paper in an airtight container.

EVERTON TOFFEE

Adapted from Mrs Beeton's *Book of Household Management* (1861)

2 non-stick shallow tins 7½″ × 7½″ (19 × 19 cm), greased
Makes about 1¼ lb (0.57 kg)

INGREDIENTS
¼ pint (150 ml) water
1 lb (450 g) granulated sugar
4 oz (100 g) butter
pinch cream of tartar
6 drops essence of lemon

METHOD
Cream the butter. Put the water and sugar into a heavy based saucepan. Dissolve the sugar gently, then bring to the boil to the soft crack stage (270°F 132°C). Remove from the heat, then stirring continuously add the creamed butter, cream of tartar and essence of lemon. Return to the heat and boil to the hard crack stage (310°F 154°C). Remove from the heat and pour the toffee into the prepared tins, when it begins to set mark the surface into squares using a buttered knife blade. Leave until cold then remove from the tins and break the toffee into the marked squares.

Make a parcel of each toffee by wrapping first in waxed paper and then with coloured metallic paper. Keep in an airtight container.

COFFEE BON-BONS
Adapted from the *Cooks Guide* by Charles Elmé Francatelli (1888)

13″ × 9″ (33 × 30 cm) Swiss roll tray lightly greased
Makes about ½ lb (225g)

INGREDIENTS
8 oz (225 g) granulated sugar
8 fl oz (225 ml) strong Camp coffee

METHOD
In a heavy based saucepan put 6 fl oz (175 ml) strong Camp coffee with the sugar. Boil to the snap (310°F 154°C) and then stir in the remainder. Continue working the composition at the side of the pan with a wooden spoon for about 5 minutes. As soon as it begins to thicken, pour it out onto prepared tray and allow it to be about 1/6″ (2 mm) deep. When it becomes set and before it cools, with the back of the blade of a knife, mark it out in oblong squares, measuring 1″ × ½″ (2.5 × 1 cm). When the bon-bons are quite cold, they will easily be snapped apart.

Make each bon-bon into a parcel by wrapping first in waxed paper and then with coloured metallic paper. Keep in an airtight container.

GREAT GRANDMOTHER'S ALMOND BRITTLE

12″ × 7″ (30 × 18 cm) tin greased
Makes about 1½ lb (700 g)

INGREDIENTS
1¼ lb (560 g) caster sugar
5 oz (125 g) flaked almonds
1½ tablespoons lemon juice

METHOD

Put the sugar and lemon juice into a heavy based saucepan. Place over a medium heat and stir continuously using a wooden spoon until the sugar has dissolved and the mixture turns a deep golden colour. Add the flaked almonds and stir in thoroughly. Remove from the heat and spread the almond brittle out quickly and evenly into the prepared tin using a hot wet knife blade. Still using the knife, mark the almond brittle into squares. Cool in fridge. When set, break it into the marked squares.

Wrap each piece of almond brittle first in waxed paper and then in coloured metallic paper. Keep in an airtight container.

GREAT GRANDMOTHER'S VANILLA FUDGE

7½″ × 7½″ (19 × 19 cm) non-stick shallow tin, greased
Makes about 1½ lb (700 g)

INGREDIENTS
1 lb (450 g) granulated sugar
2 oz (50 g) butter
½ pint (275 ml) full cream milk
1 teaspoon vanilla essence

METHOD

Place the sugar, butter and milk in a large heavy based saucepan over a gentle heat and stir until the sugar has dissolved. Bring to the boil and boil steadily (stirring frequently to prevent the mixture sticking to the bottom of the pan and burning) until the soft ball stage (235°F 113°C) is reached. Remove the pan from the heat and stir in the essence; beat until the fudge mixture is thick and creamy. Pour at once into the prepared tin. When nearly set cut into squares using a knife which has been dipped into hot water. Leave until cold then remove the fudge from the tin and break it into the marked squares.

Store for no longer than one week in a cool place using an airtight container with waxed paper between the layers of fudge.

CANDIED, CRYSTALLIZED AND GLACE FRUITS

Only perfect, firm, ripe fruit should be used. Soft fruits such as blackberries, loganberries, raspberries and strawberries do not process well. It is advisable to candy each type of fruit separately in order to keep the individual flavour. The following are some of the fruits which are suitable for crystallizing: apricots – whole, prick with a silver fork, the stones are easy to remove, cherries — stoned, grapes — deseeded, mandarins — whole, peeled, pith removed, prick fruit with a silver fork, mandarin segments, pith removed, peaches — peeled, halved and stoned, pears — peeled, quartered and cored, pineapple — peeled, cored and sliced, slices then cut into wedge shaped pieces

CANDIED FRUIT

INGREDIENTS
1 lb (450 g) fruit — prepared as indicated
4 oz (100 g) powdered glucose
2½ oz (60 g) granulated sugar
½ pint (275 ml) reserved juice — adding extra water if necessary to make up the quantity

METHOD
Place the prepared fruit in a large saucepan and cover it with boiling water. Simmer over a gentle heat until the fruit is just tender, but not broken. The time for this process will vary with the type of fruit used. Remove fruit carefully from the juice with a slotted spoon and place in a heatproof dish. Reserve the juice.

Put ½ pint (275 ml) of juice, glucose and sugar into a saucepan over a gentle heat; stir until the sugar has dissolved. Bring to the boil then pour the hot syrup over the fruit making sure the fruit is completely immersed. Cover and leave for 24 hours.

Place a sieve over a saucepan and carefully drain the syrup from the fruit into the saucepan. Return fruit to the heatproof dish. Add 2 oz (50 g) of sugar to the syrup, stir over a gentle heat until the sugar has dissolved. Bring to the boil then pour the hot syrup over the fruit. Cover and leave for 24 hours. Repeat process 3 more times.

Place a sieve over a large saucepan and carefully drain the syrup from the fruit into the saucepan. Add 3 oz (75 g) of sugar to the syrup, place saucepan over a gentle heat and stir syrup until the sugar has dissolved then add the fruit and simmer for 3 minutes. Return fruit and syrup to the heatproof dish. Cover and leave for 48 hours. Repeat. The syrup should now be as thick as clear honey.

If the syrup is too thin at this stage add another 3 oz (75 g) of sugar to the syrup; dissolve the sugar in the syrup over a gentle heat then add the fruit and simmer for 3 minutes. Leave the fruit to soak in the thick syrup for 4 days. Remove fruit carefully from the syrup with a slotted spoon and lay it on a wire rack placed over a baking tray to catch the drips.

To dry place tray containing the rack and fruit in a warm place such as an airing cupboard. Turn the fruit occasionally during the drying process. The fruit is finished when the surface is no longer sticky. At this stage the fruit is classified as candied.

CRYSTALLIZED FRUIT

INGREDIENTS
dried candied fruit
granulated sugar

METHOD
Lift each piece of dried candied fruit up with a fine skewer; quickly dip the fruit into boiling water then allow it to drain for a moment. Roll each piece of fruit in the sugar until the fruit is evenly but not thickly coated. Leave to dry on a wire rack before storing.

GLACE FRUIT

INGREDIENTS

1 lb (450 g) granulated sugar
¼ pint (150 ml) water
dried candied fruit — prepared as before

METHOD

Put the sugar and water into a saucepan over a gentle heat. When the sugar has dissolved, bring to the boil and boil for 1 minute. Pour some of the syrup into a hot cup (keeping the remaining syrup in the saucepan hot, but not boiling). Lift each piece of dried candied fruit up with a fine skewer. Quickly dip the fruit into boiling water, allow it to drain for a moment then quickly dip the fruit into the syrup. Lay the fruit on a wire rack placed over a baking tray. When the syrup in the cup becomes cloudy or too diluted replace it with fresh hot syrup from the saucepan and continue with the exercise. Place tray containing the wire rack and fruit in a warm place such as an airing cupboard. Turn the fruit occasionally during the drying process. The fruit is finished when the surface is no longer sticky.

Store in a cool, dry place in cardboard or wooden boxes which have been lined with waxed paper. The fruit should be placed well apart and between layers of waxed paper. It is important that the box is not airtight.

These fruits are best if eaten within 6 months.

CURAÇAO TRUFFLES

A large tray covered in greaseproof paper
Makes about 1½ lb (700 g)

INGREDIENTS
6 oz (175 g) plain chocolate
2 oz (50 g) soft butter
1 orange
4 oz (100 g) ground almonds
12 oz (350 g) icing sugar
3 tablespoons Curaçao
desiccated coconut

METHOD
Grate the chocolate and put in a bowl over a saucepan of hot water (do not let the bowl touch the water). Stir the chocolate until it has just melted then remove the bowl from the heat. Add the butter to the melted chocolate and blend the two ingredients together. Finely grate the orange and stir the rind, ground almond, icing sugar and the Curaçao into the chocolate/butter mixture until thoroughly blended. Remove the mixture a teaspoonful at a time and then form each teaspoonful into a ball. Roll each ball in dessicated coconut. Arrange truffles on the prepared tray and leave to dry for a few hours.

These will keep for about one month if placed between layers of waxed paper and stored in an airtight container. Serve in petits-fours paper cases.

GREAT GRANDMOTHER'S FRUITS FARCIES

INGREDIENTS
soft almond paste (see page 17)
dried candied cherries (see page 154)
dried candied grapes

METHOD
Roll soft almond paste into small balls between clean hands. Cut each fruit in half lengthways. Place one almond paste ball between the cut halves of each fruit. Sandwich the almond paste between the fruit halves by very gently pressing the fruit halves onto almond paste.

Serve in petits fours paper cases. These should be eaten on the day they are made.

ORANGE CREAMS

Makes about 1 lb 2 oz (500 g)

INGREDIENTS
1 medium sized orange
1½ tablespoons Curaçao
1 lb 2 oz (500 g) (approximately) icing sugar

METHOD
Grate rind from orange and extract juice. Place grated orange rind/juice and Curaçao in a large bowl. Add sufficient sifted icing sugar to form a firm paste. The amount of icing sugar required depends upon the size of the orange that is used. Knead well then turn paste out onto a working surrace which has been lightly dusted with sifted icing sugar. Sift icing sugar over the paste then roll out to about ¼″ (6 mm) thick. Cut into 1″ (25 mm) rounds. Place on greaseproof paper and leave to dry for about 24 hours. Line an airtight container with waxed paper and place orange creams between layers of waxed paper.

PEPPERMINT CREAMS

Makes about 1 lb (450 g)

INGREDIENTS
1 lb (450 g) icing sugar
1 large egg
few drops oil of peppermint

METHOD

Separate egg and lightly whisk egg white. Sift icing sugar. Place icing sugar in a large bowl and mix in the egg white and oil of peppermint. Work into a firm paste. Knead well then turn paste out onto a working surface which has been lightly dusted with sifted icing sugar. Sift icing sugar over the paste then roll out to about ¼″ (6 mm) thick. Cut into 1″ (25 mm) rounds. Place rounds on greaseproof paper and leave to dry for about 24 hours. Line an airtight container with waxed paper and place peppermint creams between layers of waxed paper.

ROSEWATER CREAMS

INGREDIENTS

1 lb (450 g) icing sugar
2 tablespoons single cream
2 tablespoons rose water
1 medium egg

METHOD

Separate egg and lightly whisk egg white. Sift icing sugar. Place icing sugar in a large bowl and mix in the single cream, rose water and egg white. Work into a firm paste. Knead well then turn paste out onto a working surface which has been lightly dusted with sifted icing sugar. Sift icing sugar over the paste then roll out to about ¼″ (6 mm) thick. Cut into 1″ (25 mm) rounds. Place rounds on greaseproof paper and leave to dry for about 24 hours. Line an airtight container with waxed paper and place rosewater creams between layers of waxed paper.

GREAT GRANDMOTHER'S STUFFED DATES ENROBED WITH MARZIPAN

INGREDIENTS

dessert dates
1 whole almond to each date
½ oz (10 g) soft marzipan to each date
caster sugar

METHOD

Make a slit in the dates lengthways and remove the stones. Blanche, skin and lightly toast almonds under grill or in oven. Fill each date hollow with a cold toasted almond. Mould marzipan around each nut stuffed date covering the date completely. Then roll in caster sugar.

GREAT GRANDMOTHER'S RUM TURKISH DELIGHT

8″ × 6″ (20 × 15 cm) non-stick tin wetted with cold water
Makes about 1¼ lb (560 g)

INGREDIENTS

1 lb (450 g) granulated sugar
9 fl oz (250 ml) cold water
1 orange
1 lemon
1 oz (25 g) powdered gelatine
1 tablespoon rum
2 oz (50 g) chopped nuts
icing sugar

METHOD

Grate the orange and lemon rinds and extract juice. Place the sugar, 9 fl oz of cold water, orange/lemon rinds and juice in a pan. Stir and heat gently to dissolve the sugar. Sprinkle gelatine onto 4 tablespoons (60 ml) cold water, stir and leave a few minutes to sponge. Add the sponged gelatine stirring constantly, simmer until gelatine has dissolved (when a metal spoon is lifted out and is free of granules). Boil gently for 20 minutes then strain through a sieve into a bowl and add the rum. Let the mixture remain in the bowl until on the point of setting then stir in the nuts and pour at once into the prepared tin and leave for 24 hours in a cold place. When perfectly set turn the jelly out and cut it into 1″ (2.5 cm) squares then roll the squares in the sifted icing sugar. Line an airtight container with waxed paper and place the Turkish delight between layers of waxed paper. Sprinkle each layer of Turkish delight with sifted icing sugar.

GREAT GRANDMOTHER'S PEPPERMINT TURKISH DELIGHT

8″ × 6″ (20 × 15 cm) non-stick tin wetted with cold water
Makes about 1 lb (450 g)

INGREDIENTS

1 lb (450 g) granulated sugar
9 fl oz (250 ml) cold water
1 oz (25 g) powdered gelatine
few drops oil of peppermint — to taste
a few drops green food colouring
icing sugar

METHOD

Place the sugar and the 9 fl oz of cold water in a pan, stir and heat gently to dissolve the sugar. Sprinkle gelatine on 4 tablespoons of cold water, stir and leave a few minutes to sponge. Add the sponged gelatine to the pan stirring constantly, simmer until gelatine has dissolved (when a metal spoon is lifted out of the mixture and is free of granules). Boil gently for 20 minutes. Add the oil of peppermint and green food colouring. Pour into the prepared tin and leave for 24 hours in a cold place. When perfectly set turn the jelly out, cut it into 1″ (2.5 cm) squares then roll the squares in the sifted icing sugar. Line an airtight container with waxed paper and place the Turkish delight between layers of waxed paper. Sprinkle each layer of Turkish delight with sifted icing sugar.

Note: Rose Turkish Delight can be made by sprinkling the gelatine on 1 tablespoon of rosewater mixed with 3 tablespoons of cold water. Allow to sponge and continue the recipe as before adding a further tablespoon of rosewater and a few drops of pink food colouring in place of the peppermint and green food colouring.

FROSTED HOLLY LEAVES

Adapted from Mrs Beeton's *Book of Household Management* (1861)
These are used as a decoration for dessert and supper dishes

INGREDIENTS
sprigs of holly
clarified butter
caster sugar

METHOD

Pick the holly leaves from the stalks and wipe them with a clean cloth free from all moisture. Place leaves on a sheet of greaseproof paper and leave in a warm place to dry out thoroughly. When dry, but not shrivelled, paint each leaf lightly all over with clarified butter, then dust with caster sugar. Place finished leaves onto wire rack covered with a sheet of greaseproof paper and leave to dry in a warm place.

They should be kept in a dry place until ready for use.

FROSTED MINT LEAVES

INGREDIENTS
mint leaves
1 small egg white — lightly beaten
caster sugar

METHOD

Brush each leaf liberally all over with egg white then dust with caster sugar. Place finished leaves onto the prepared wire rack and leave in a warm place until dry to the touch.

Stored in an airtight container between layers of waxed paper they will keep for a year or more.

DECORATIONS

Children love to join in the Christmas preparations, making toys for the tree is great fun. Pieces of old cardboard, shoe boxes, felt tip pens, pipe cleaners, felt, kitchen foil, old beads, plasticine, wool, sweet wrappers and cotton wool can all be used in place of the items shown. Hunting for alternatives can add to the fun. Papier mâché can be used for anything that requires a mould. All the items can be bought from craft shops.

CHRISTMAS CRACKERS FOR THE FESTIVE TABLE

One of the advantages of making your own Christmas crackers is that each guest will receive a special gift from the contents of their cracker which has been personally chosen for them. You can also make them any size you wish.

    You can follow our instructions for making your crackers or cheat a little by buying a cheap box of crackers and very carefully remove the outer paper and motif. Then re-cover the cardboard tubes with a new cover and motif of your choice. By adopting this method you are able to use the paper hats, mottos and snaps which come with the crackers. Then discard the original gifts and replace them with specially selected gifts. Then we finish off the cracker by covering the gathered sections at each end with ribbon.

    The materials needed for making Christmas crackers can be found at most art shops.

MATERIALS

scissors
8" × 6½" (20 × 16 cm) thin card
9" × 6½" (22.5 × 16 cm) lining paper/typing paper
clear glue
snapper
15" × 7" (38 × 18 cm) crepe paper
23" × 4½" (58 × 12 cm) tissue paper for hat
hand written or printed motto
gift
lace and ribbon to decorate
thin cord

METHOD

Lay out the crepe paper on a flat working surface and place the thin sheet of lining paper/typing paper in the centre. Then place the snapper (the thin strip that makes the bang) along the length of the lining paper. Cut the card into three sections and glue each onto the lining paper (over the snapper) to allow a 1" gap between them, as indicated on the diagram. Place gift, hat and motto in the centre tube, glue the entire edge of one side and carefully roll up the crepe paper and contents to form the cracker (see facing diagrams) taking care to hold the glued edge down for a few moments to avoid it unrolling. Seal off the middle section by tying each end firmly with thin cord; then cover this with red ribbon for decoration. Using clear glue you can now decorate the cracker with lace – for added security you can sew the lace cuffs onto each end – and finally add the centre decoration to complete the cracker.

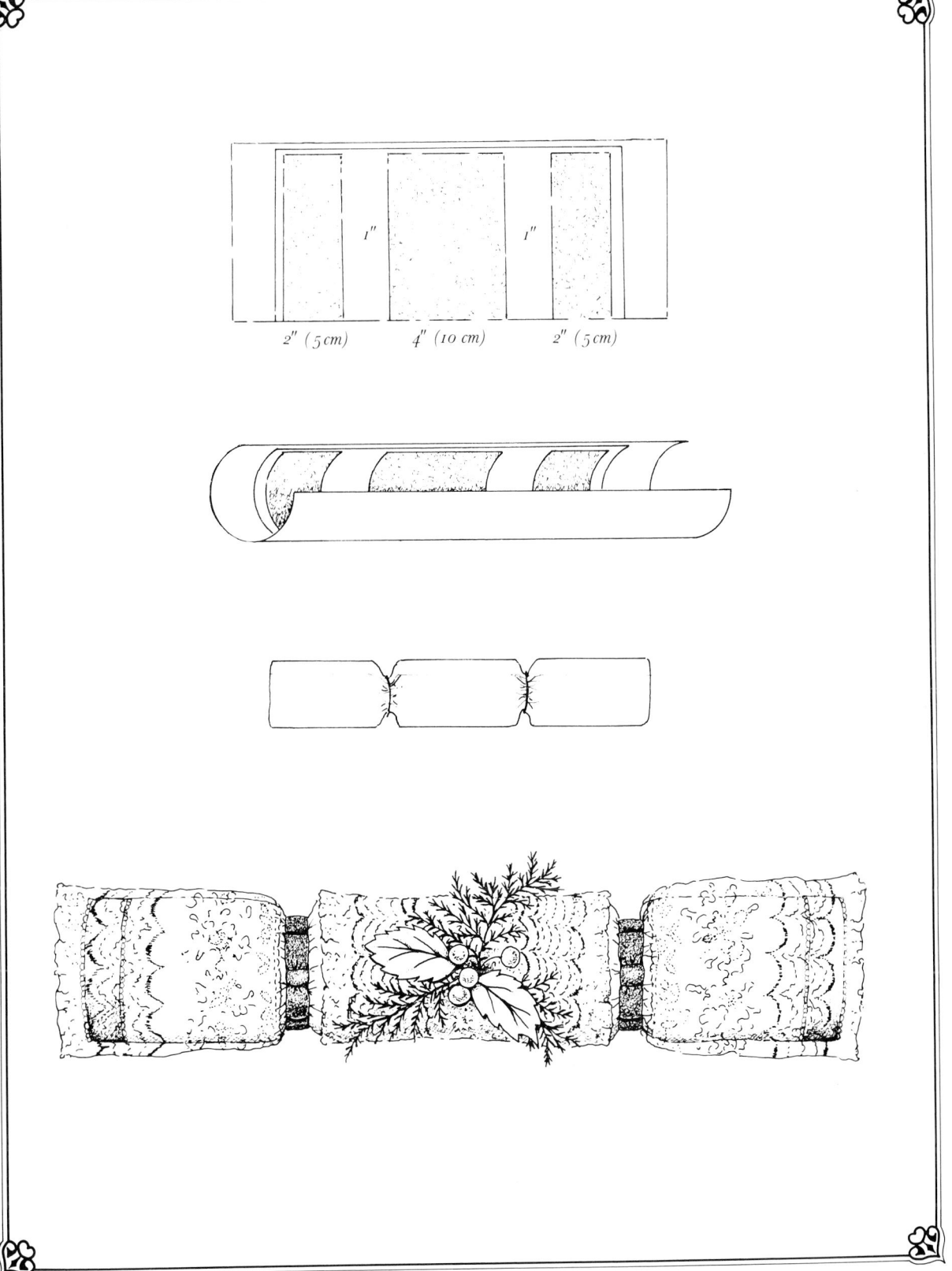

1"   1"

2" (5 cm)   4" (10 cm)   2" (5 cm)

CHRISTMAS SERVIETTE RING

MATERIALS

kitchen or toilet roll tube
glue
scissors
white ribbon — 2″ (5 cm) wide
red ribbon — 1″ (2.5 cm) wide
lace — ½″ (1 cm) wide
lace — 1″ (2.5 cm) wide
silver leaves
red flowers
silver balls

METHOD

Cut cardboard tube to 2″ (5 cm) in length. Wrap the white ribbon around the tube allowing 2″ (5 cm) extra and cut. Fold 1″ of the ribbon back and glue so there is 1″ of double thickness, when dry cut a 'V' in end of ribbon. Cover the outside of the tube with glue and very carefully cover with white ribbon, do not glue the V down — this should overlap. Glue the red ribbon on the top of the white and starting at the top of the V take this around the tube and tuck the end under the V. Press down and leave to dry. Glue around outside edge of tube, press the narrow lace onto this allowing it to overhang, leave to dry. Repeat using 1″ (2.5 cm) lace. At the centre of the V, glue the silver leaves, silver balls, and red flowers, leave to dry. Roll serviette and insert.

Note: The silver leaves may be cut from kitchen foil.

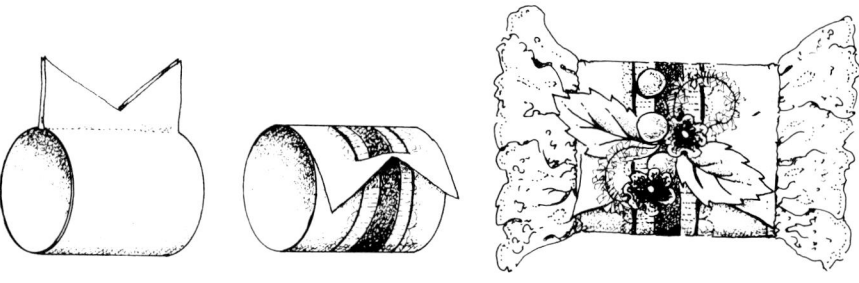

VICTORIAN CHRISTMAS TREE CARDS

With a little added lace and ribbon Victorian style Christmas cards, with hand written greetings on the back, make attractive and interesting tree decorations.

MATERIALS
scissors
clear glue
Victorian style Christmas cards
lace
ribbon

METHOD

Measure around the edge of the card, cut 2 lengths of lace or lace and ribbon (making an allowance for turning the corners). Cut a length of ribbon to form a loop; glue the 2 cut ends of the loop onto the top of the card at the back. Glue card edges lightly and attach the chosen trim around the back and front edges. Leave to dry.

CHRISTMAS TABLE CENTRE PIECE

MATERIALS

plastic or glass container 5″ × 7″ wide (12 × 17 cm), depth 2½″ (6 cm)
florist foam
scissors
florist sticky tape
holly and fern
2 No. 9 (8 cm) candles red
red ribbon ¾″ (2 cm) wide, 17″ (43 cm) long
Christmas roses real, silk, or plastic
sprigs of mistletoe real, silk, or plastic
florist wires
fine wire
4 baubles red

METHOD

Cut florist foam to fit container allow 1½″ (4 cm) of foam above container.

Take the florist tape and secure one end of the base of the container, bring the tape over the top of one end of foam and down again to the base, secure and cut. Repeat on the other side. This will stop the foam from moving.

Put the container with foam in under the tap and let the cold water run on the foam for about 3 minutes, remove and pour off excess water.

Cut off 2 long pieces of fern and gently push 1 in each side of the foam, cut 2 more slightly smaller and push these in just above, make sure they are pointing downwards and flat, now work on the back and front. They should be shorter than the sides, but also pointing down and flat, (you are really hiding the container and foam). Keep building the fern until you have filled all the sides.

Take the 2 candles and push them gently into the foam diagonally opposite each other. (Do not move from side to side or you may crack the foam.)

Cut ribbon in half, and fold into 4 loops, secure at the bottom with fine wire, cut a small length of florist wire and attach it to the base of the ribbon, push this in the foam at the base of candle. Repeat for the second candle.

Push the sprigs of holly into the middle of the arrangement. You should not be able to see the container or foam.

Now for the finishing touches. Push in the sprigs of mistletoe, Christmas roses and red baubles as shown, if the stems are not long enough lengthen with florist wire and tape. Pour water into containers be sure not to over fill.

This arrangement should last about a week. Dampen the foam if it feels dry to the touch.

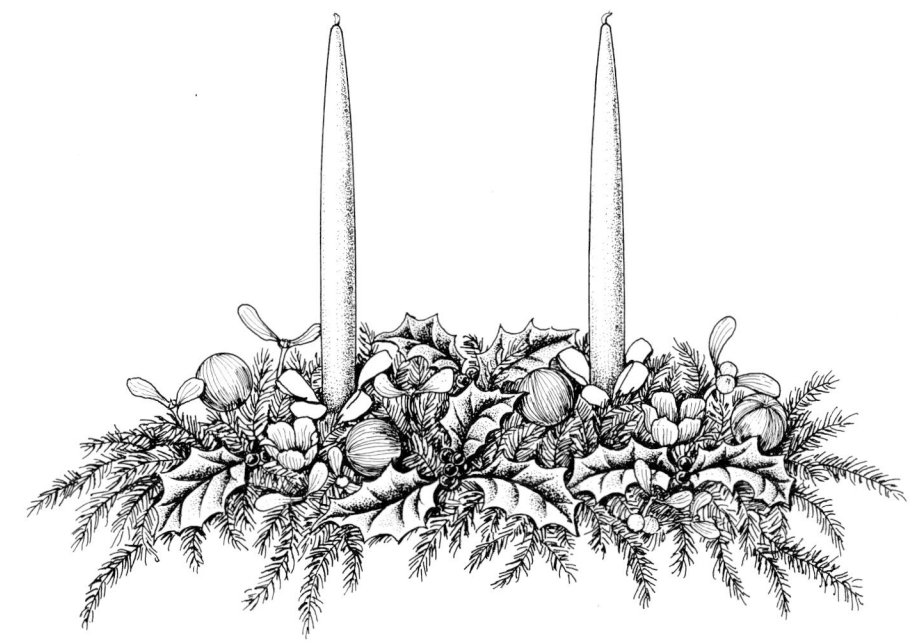

HOLLY AND MISTLETOE RING

MATERIALS
12" wire frame covered in moss
sprigs of holly
sprigs of mistletoe
packet of florist wires
artificial Christmas roses
red ribbon — 1" (2.5 cm) wide
red ribbon ½" (1 cm) wide
artificial red berries
fine wire
stapler

METHOD

If the moss is dry dampen slightly and leave over night. Secure the sprigs of holly and mistletoe all around the wire ring, leave 4 small spaces for the ribbon.

Take the 1" ribbon and cut 4 equal lengths, remember that this will be hanging, so you don't want them to be long.

Loop the end of each piece of ribbon around the ring and secure with the stapler. Make sure the ribbons are still the same length or it will not hang straight.

Cut equal lengths of the ½" (1 cm) ribbon enough for 4 bows with long tails to hang below the ring, now secure one bow on the ribbons.

Make a loop with the wire, then pull 2 of the long ribbons through the wire ring then secure the 4 ends with the stapler.

Fill in any spaces between the holly and the mistletoe with the Christmas roses and berries.

Using the ½" (1 cm) ribbon make several loops and secure in the middle with wire, then add 4 tails to hang down, secure this to the top of the long ribbons so you hide the wire loop.

HOLLY RING

MATERIALS
12" (30 cm) wire frame covered with moss
sprigs of holly
clear varnish
paint brush
walnuts
pine cones
artificial red berries
packet of soft florist wire
large red ribbon bow
fine wire

METHOD

If moss is dry dampen slightly and leave over night so excess water has gone. Fold a length of wire in half, then make a hole in the base of each walnut and push the bent end into the hole, the nut will keep the wire in place, open the 2 ends they will be needed to secure the walnut to the frame. Wind the wire around the cones above the lowest layer of scales leave enough wire to secure them to the frame. Varnish each walnut and cone and leave over night to dry. Starting at the top of the frame secure the first sprig of holly with the fine wire, keep the stems downwards then each time you add a sprig of holly the leaves will cover the stems. When all the holly has been secured you can now start to insert the walnuts and the cones; you can wire 2 or 3 cones together or 1 walnut and 2 cones then secure them to the frame, make small bunches of the red berries and secure them to the frame also. Make a loop on the top of the frame with wire — this must be strong enough to take the weight of the holly ring. Fix the red bow at the top of the frame.

CHRISTMAS PUDDING

MATERIALS
3″ (7.5 cm) round plastic mould — old bauble or tennis ball
small sprig of holly
brown acrylic paint
white acrylic paint
meat skewer
6″ (15 cm) of gold cord
palette knife
freshly ground black pepper

METHOD
Push the tip of the meat skewer into the top of the ball, this will act as a handle while you paint the ball. Cover the ball completely with brown paint, while the paint is still wet sprinkle with the black pepper, leave to dry. Squeeze the white paint onto the top of the ball and let it run down the sides to resemble cream, smooth the paint over the top with the palette knife and also down the sides, this will take longer to dry so leave it overnight. Remove the skewer, put glue into the hole and push the two ends of the gold cord in followed by the stem of the sprig of holly, push down hard then leave to dry.

Note: The Christmas Pudding can be made using papier mâché for which you need a large bowl, lots of old newspaper or soft paper and 1 pint (600 ml) water. Put the water in the bowl, tear the paper into thin strips and immerse in the bowl for 3–4 hours. Then squeeze all the water out of the paper and mould into a ball. Leave until it has dried out completely.

SILVER MEDALLION

MATERIALS
scissors
glue
cardboard
silver crepe paper
red sequin leaves
silver glitter
6″ (15 cm) of silver cord
2 small spigs of holly as used for cake decoration

METHOD

Cut out 2 patterns. Cover one side of each round with glue, cover each one with silver crepe paper, trim edges neatly. Spread glue on the edge of each round and sprinkle with glitter, leave to dry. Cover one side of one round with glue, then with the glue on the inside press the two together, before pressing the tops together insert the two ends of silver cord make sure the loop is straight, while the glue is wet insert the red leaves all around the edge, keep the pointed ends on the outside, press down hard, if you have a heavy book leave this on the top until dry. Make a small hole in the centre of the round and insert one stem of holly, turn the round over and put glue into the hole then insert the stem of the second sprig of holly, hang up to dry.

FATHER CHRISTMAS

MATERIALS
cardboard
scissors
red and gold glitter
black red and blue acrylic paint or felt tip pens
white, black and flesh colour felt
paint brush
cotton wool
gold paper
glue
6" (15 cm) of gold cord
gossamer tree floss

METHOD
Trace off 2 Father Christmas patterns and cut out in cardboard. Cover one side of one Father Christmas with glue and press both figures together starting at the bottom. Before you press the tops together insert the 2 ends of gold cord. Make sure the loop is straight, then press down hard and leave to dry. Trace off and cut out 2 teddy bear patterns. Cut out in cardboard and cover one side of one bear with glue except for one arm, press the 2 together and leave to dry. With the black felt cut out 2 belts and 2 right and left boots. Use white felt to make the fur trims on his hat, cuffs, bottom of jacket and tops of his boots. Cut out one pattern for the face in the flesh-coloured felt. Cover one side of the bear with glue and sprinkle with gold glitter, repeat on the other side. Now trace all the outlines for Father Christmas's clothes onto the cutout and on one side cover all the areas for his red suit and hat with glue. Sprinkle with red glitter and allow to dry before repeating on his back. Paint a face onto the felt with the paints giving him a round red mouth and don't forget to add a bit of colour to his cheeks. To make a moustache roll a piece of cotton wool between your fingers and glue onto the felt. You can now glue the face into position on the cutout and add a blob of paint for the nose. Leave to dry. Now glue on his boots, belt and all the white trimmings. To make his beard, pull off small amounts of tree floss (or cotton wool) and stick them into place until his beard looks long and bushy. Cut a buckle out of gold paper and stick into place. Now glue the inside of the teddy bear's arm and press this onto Father Christmas's hands. Paint his hands black and paint in the eyes and nose of the teddy bear. Once dry you can gently brush all the white felt with an old toothbrush to make it look like fur.

CHRISTMAS TREE

MATERIALS
scissors
glue
cardboard
6" (15 cm) of gold cord
green glitter
coloured sequins
2 silver star sequins

METHOD

Cut out 2 tree patterns. Cover one side of one tree with glue. With glue on the inside press the two trees together starting at the bottom, before pressing the tops together insert the two ends of the gold cord, make sure the loop is straight, press down hard then leave to dry. Cover sides of the tree with glue then sprinkle with glitter until covered, leave to dry — do one side at a time. Put glue all around the outer edges and sprinkle with glitter, then leave to dry. Glue coloured sequins on both sides then leave to dry. Glue a silver star on the top of the tree on both sides then hang up to dry.

HOLLY SQUARE

MATERIALS
red felt
pinking shears
6" (15 cm) of gold cord
14" (35 cm) of narrow gold braid
4 long green chenille covered wires 12" (30 cm)
8 very small red chenille covered balls
glue

METHOD

Cut out 2 red felt squares 3¾ × 3¾" (9.5 × 9.5 cm). Cover one side of one square with glue then press the two squares together, insert the two ends of gold cord into one corner while the glue is still wet, press down hard then leave to dry. When dry cut round the edge with the pinking shears. Glue the braid around the border of the square on each side, keep as near the edge as possible, leave to dry. Take one length of covered wire, fold in half and make into 2 loops twist to secure, now gently pull each loop open and form into a holly leaf shape. Repeat on other square, then glue them both together in the centre. Do same for remaining side. Put glue on the back of each holly sprig and glue one to each side of the felt in the centre, make sure the tip of each leaf is pointing to each corner of the square, leave to dry. Glue the 4 red balls in the centre of each holly sprig, then hang up to dry.

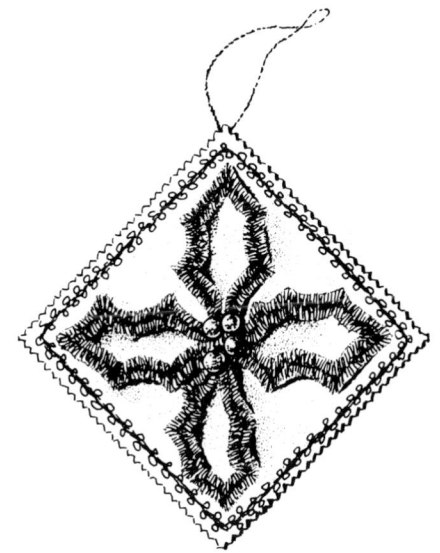

PEG SOLDIER

MATERIALS
1 old fashioned dolly peg
acrylic paint — black, blue white and red
paint brush
white felt
black felt
6 small gold beads
gold cord
glue

METHOD
On the top of the peg paint the face on the front, and the hair on the back, leave to dry. Starting at the neck paint 1½" (4 cm) down with the red paint, then 1" (2.5 cm) in white paint and the final 1" (2.5 cm) in black paint, leave to dry. Cut a length of white felt 3½" (9 cm) long, ¾" (2 cm) wide, fold in half lengthways, cut 4" (10 cm) off the pipe cleaner, spread glue on inside of the felt and insert the pipe cleaner, now press the felt together, when dry paint the felt red, leave to dry. Cut a narrow strip of black felt and stick this around his black waist, then cut 2 narrower strips and stick on the top of the black boots, leave to dry. Stick the 6 beads on the front of his red jacket, 3 each side, leave to dry. Cut a narrow strip of white felt and stick this diagonally across his chest, leave to dry. Bend the pipe cleaner in half and stick the centre onto the back of the jacket and bring the arms to the front, leave to dry. To make hat, cut a length of black felt 1" (2.5 cm) wide, 2¼" (6 cm) long, glue the ends together, when dry cut a small round of black felt to fit the top of the hat, glue this on the top. Stick the hat on his head, then stick gold cord around his neck, and a length from the hat to go under the chin. Make a small gold buckle out of paper and stick onto the belt.

(i)　　　　　(ii)　　　　　(iii)

(iv)　　　　　(v)

MISS PEGGY

MATERIALS
1 old fashioned dolly peg
acrylic paint or felt tip pen — brown, red and blue
paint brush
brown raffia or wool
red and white felt
thin cardboard
pipe cleaner
glue

METHOD

Paint or draw a face on front of peg. Leave to dry. Cut out cardboard templates. Cut out coat, hat, sleeves and cape from templates in red felt. Glue the cardboard around the peg so you can stand the peg up. Leave to dry. Cover the cardboard with the red felt to start the coat. Leave to dry. Cut 4″ (10 cm) off the pipe cleaner, spread glue on inside of felt and insert the pipe cleaner. Now press the felt together. Leave to dry. Bend the pipe cleaner in half and stick the centre onto the back of the top of the coat and bring the arms to the front, leave to dry. Glue white trim around edge of cape, and collar around her neck and strip of white felt for opening. Wind white felt around her hands and glue to make a muff. Leave to dry. Glue the cape around her neck and pinch 2 pleats on the top of each sleeve and glue. Leave to dry. Glue her hair on the back of head, leave long so it can be tied back. Leave to dry. Glue red felt on her head and stick white trim around edge. Leave to dry.

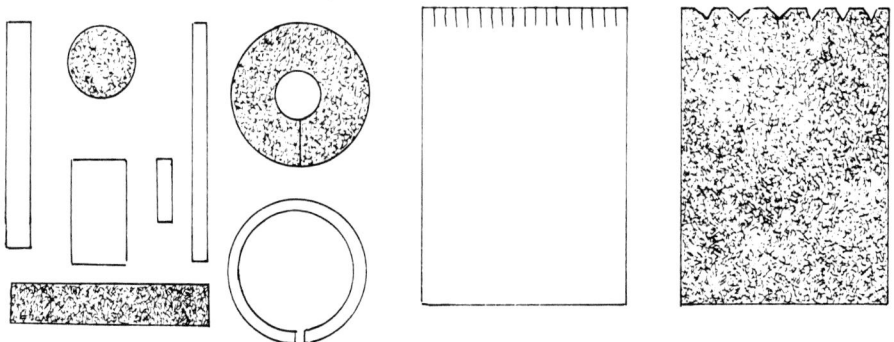

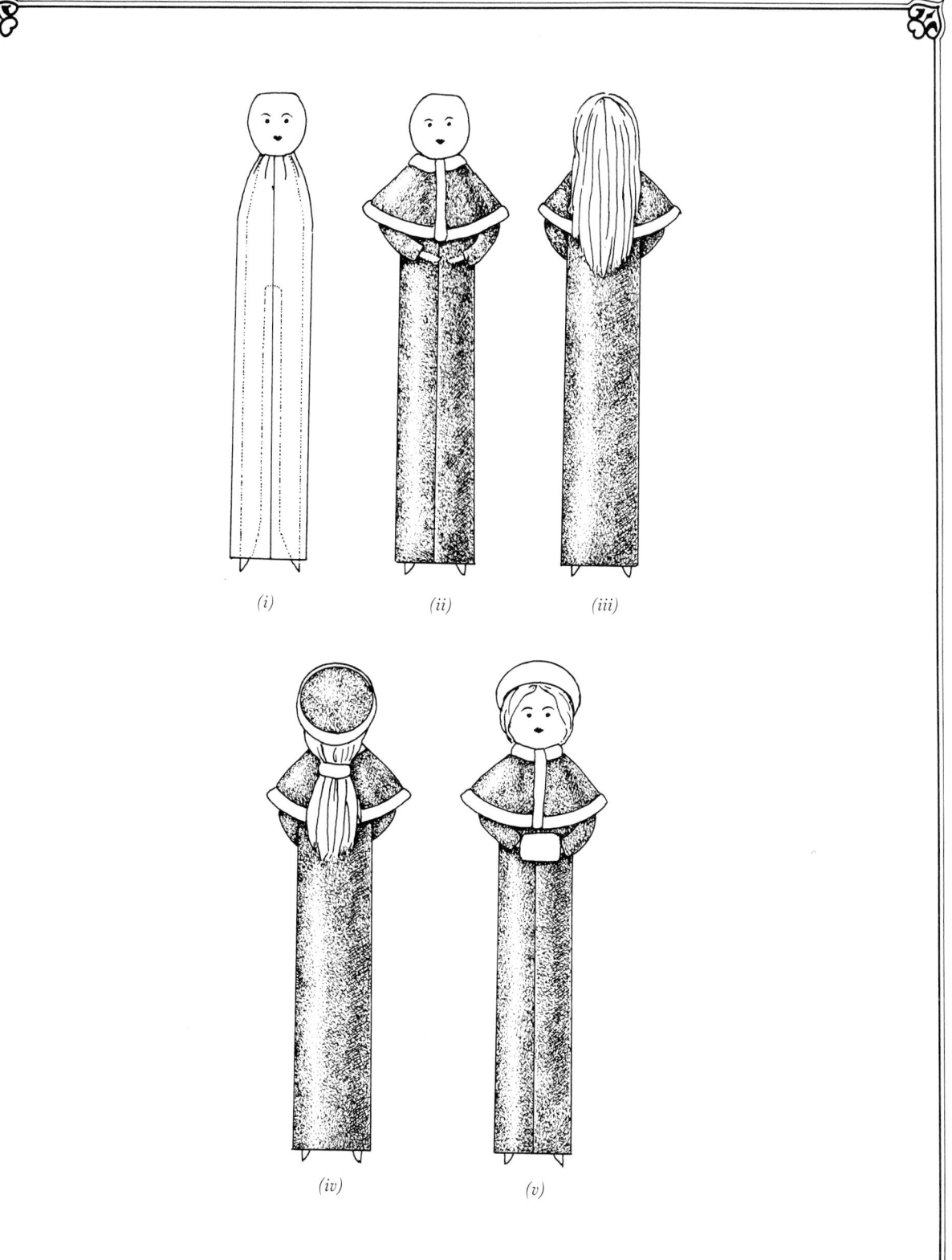

(i)   (ii)   (iii)

(iv)   (v)

JOEY THE CLOWN

MATERIALS

scissors
cardboard (white on one side)
glue
red, white and black acrylic paint
various colours of glitter and acrylic paint
6" (15 cm) of cord
pencil
paint brush

METHOD

Cut out 2 clown patterns. Put glue on the brown side of one clown then press the 2 clowns together, make sure the 2 brown sides are on the inside, before pressing the tops together insert the 2 ends of cord, press down hard and leave to dry. Trace all the markings from the pattern onto both sides of the clown. Paint the boots with the black paint on both sides and the hands and face with white paint, hang up to dry. The face is the same on both sides, just a cross for each eye with the black paint and a red nose. Using the red paint give him a big smile. For the clowns costume use the acrylic paint but it must be thin enough to see the traced lines through, if you wish to use glitter sprinkle on while the paint is still wet, you can paint the costume in any colour, the brighter the better. For the ball paint your own design, but make each side different as you did for the costume, this can be fun to make so use your imagination you are sure to enjoy it.

ROBIN IN CAGE

MATERIALS

3 yards (277 cm) gold florist ribbon
4 red chenille covered wires 12" (30 cm)
fuse wire
scissors
blunt knife
cotton wool
small robin
glue

METHOD

Lay 2 of the red covered wires onto a flat surface to form a cross, repeat this with the other 2 then place one on top of the other to form a star, secure them with fuse wire in the centre. Gather the 8 ends together and secure with fuse wire, this is the top of the cage. Cut 3' (92 cm) off the ribbon, then tear in half lengthways and using one half secure this to the top of the cage to form a loop, this is for hanging the cage, keep the other length. Cut the remaining ribbon in half, then holding the ribbon in the centre form it into approximately 9 loops, secure this to the top of the cage. With scissors nick the top of each loop then gently pull the ribbon apart down to the wire, this will make a pom pom, you can make the strands as thin as you please. Repeat only this time include the length of ribbon laid aside. Cut this into 3 lengths, include this in the pom pom but do not form into loops, secure to the bottom of the cage. Using the long strands only, tear each strand apart lengthways up to the pom pom, then with the blunt edge of the knife hold the ribbon against the thumb and pull downwards, this will give the ribbon a curl. Glue some cotton wool in the bottom of the cage, when dry glue the robin onto the cotton wool, then hang up to dry.

Note: This can be made with pipe cleaners, but it will be much smaller. You could use a robin cake decoration and much thinner ribbon.

RED AND GOLD HEART

MATERIALS
scissors
glue
cardboard
red felt
gold ribbon
gold glitter
6″ (15 cm) of gold cord

METHOD

Cut out 2 heart patterns. Cover one side of each heart with glue and then cover with red felt, leave to dry. Cut 2 lengths of ribbon 3½″ (9 cm) long, place diagonally across each covered side of the hearts, glue each end to edge of heart, leave to dry. Cover one side of heart with glue. With glue on inside press the 2 hearts together starting at the bottom, before pressing the tops together insert the 2 ends of gold cord, make sure the loop is straight, press down hard. Cover edge of heart with glue and sprinkle with gold glitter, then hang up to dry.

SMALL SILVER STAR

MATERIALS

scissors
cardboard
glue
silver crepe paper
6" (15 cm) of silver cord
silver tinsel
double sided sticky tape
2 small sprigs of holly

METHOD

Cut out 2 star patterns. Cover one side of each star with glue and cover with silver paper, fold all the edges over neatly. Stick the sticky tape onto a flat surface then peel off the top cover and press the tinsel on the top, now very carefully press the tape onto the uncovered side of the star so that the tinsel is showing all around the edge of the star. Carefully cut the tinsel to give a short fringe all around the edges of the star. Cover the back of the other star with glue then press the two stars together starting at the bottom. Before pressing the tops together insert the two ends of silver cord, make sure the loop is straight, press down hard then leave to dry. Make a hole in the centre of the star, insert the stem of the sprig of holly then turn the star over and put glue into the hole then insert the stem of the second sprig of holly, hang up to dry.

HOLLY OVAL

MATERIALS
1 red 12" (30 cm) long chenille covered wire
2 green 12" (30 cm) long chenille covered wires
glue
6" (15 cm) of gold cord
18" (45 cm) of narrow gold braid
6 very small red chenille covered balls

METHOD
Bring the 2 ends of the red covered wire together and secure, gently pull into an oval shape. Tie the gold cord onto the top of the oval loop. Using the gold braid glue one end to the top of the oval, now wind the braid around the red covered wire until you reach the top again then secure with glue. Fold one of the green covered wires in half and make into a double loop. Twist to secure, now very gently pull each loop open and form into a holly leaf shape. Fold the second wire in half and make a loop out of one half only. Twist to secure, open the loop as before and form into a holly leaf, the straight wire is the stem, with this wind once around the centre of the other 2 leaves then bend the end of the stem over the top of the oval. Put glue on the tip of each leaf and gently hold against the inside of the oval. Glue the 3 red balls in the centre on both sides of the holly. Hang up to dry.

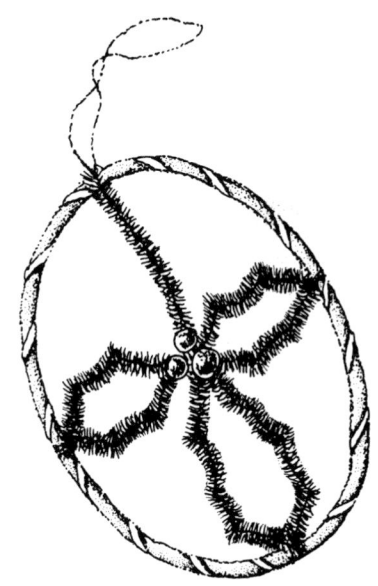

GOLD BELL

MATERIALS
scissors
glue
cardboard
gold glitter
6" (15 cm) of thin gold cord
11" (28 cm) of round gold cord
3" (7.5 cm) of red chenille covered wire
large red berry

METHOD

Cut out 2 bell patterns. Cover one side of one bell with glue then starting at the bottom press the 2 bells together, before pressing the tops together insert the 2 ends of the thin cord, make sure the loop is straight, press down hard then leave to dry. Trace a line to make the lip of the bell on both sides of the bell. Cover one side of the bell with glue but leave the traced line clear, sprinkle the glued part with gold glitter then leave to dry. Repeat on other side. Cut 4" (10 cm) off the round gold cord and glue onto the bottom edge of the bell, leave to dry. Using half of the remaining gold cord, glue this on the traced line, then repeat on the other side. Cut the red covered wire in half and glue one piece at the bottom centre of the bell just below the gold cord, repeat this on the other side, when dry glue the red berry onto the end of the wires. Hang up to dry.

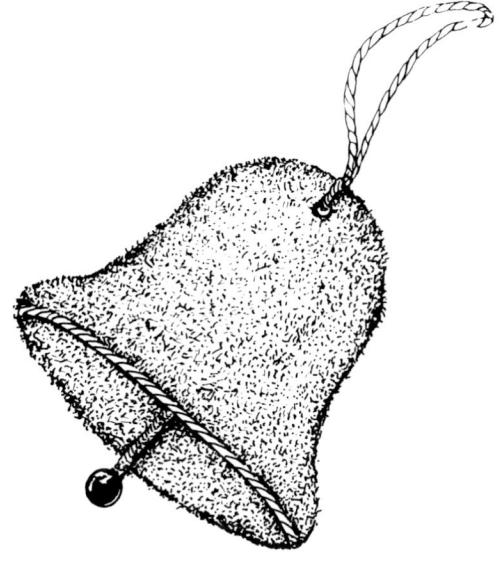

FATHER CHRISTMAS STOCKING

MATERIALS

scissors
clear glue
sewing needle
red thread
18" square (46 cm) of red felt and red and white striped cotton fabric
lace
ribbon
2½" (6.5 cm) square flesh coloured felt
4½" (11.5 cm) square white felt
acrylic paints or felt pen for faces and hoods — white, blue, red and black
cotton wood bud

METHOD

Stitch the red felt stocking together around the edge on the right side (the outer side) of the stocking; leaving the top edge of the stocking open. Stitch the cotton stocking together in the same manner as the felt stocking but this time stitching on the wrong side of the material. Insert the cotton stocking into the felt stocking. Stitch the top of the cotton stocking edge to the top of the felt stocking edge. Turn the inside top of the stocking over to form a 4" (10 cm) striped cuff. Stitching right through the four layers of material, attach a loop of ribbon onto the top edge of the back of the cuff on the outside. Trim top and bottom edges of cuff by sewing on lace and ribbon. Stitch a large ribbon bow on the front of the lower half of the cuff.

Following the Father Christmas motif diagram glue the pieces of felt for each motif together. Dip the point of the sewing needle into the white paint and paint eyebrows onto each face applying a few layers of paint (no need to wait for the paint to dry) so that the eyebrows stand out in relief. Wipe the needle clean with a damp cloth then dip the point into the blue paint and make blue dots for the eyes; clean the needle. Dip the point of the needle into the red paint to make a large red dot for each nose (building up the paint in the same manner as used for the eyebrows) until the dots resemble small red beads. Make a tiny red line for each mouth; clean the needle. Leave paint to dry. To create a cherry cheeked effect, apply a very small amount of red paint with the point of the needle to each cheek; clean the needle. Dampen the cotton wool bud and working quickly but gently rub the red paint with the dampened bud over the cheek areas. Gently tease each white felt beard and moustache with the point of the needle for the hair. Dip the point of the needle into the black paint and make tiny 'v' marks along the length of each white felt hood trim to resemble ermine tails. Edge the hood trims still using the point of the needle with a thin line of black paint; clean the needle. Glue one motif onto each side of the cuff.

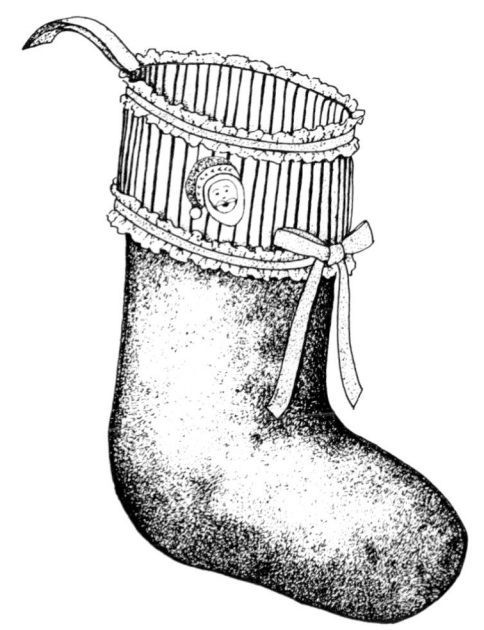

ACKNOWLEDGEMENTS

The publishers would like to thank the Mary Evans Picture Library for their kind permission to use the illustrations on pages 2, 18, 67, 70, 100, 114 and 144 and the back cover.

INDEX

A VICTORIAN CHRISTMAS